MW01155436

quilted
bags & purses

Mary Jo Hiney

STERLING/CHAPELLE
An imprint of Sterling Publishing Co., Inc.

New York / London
www.sterlingpublishing.com

Chapelle, Ltd., Inc.,
    P.O. Box 9252, Ogden, UT 84409
    (801) 621-2777 • (801) 621-2788 Fax
    e-mail: chapelle@chapelleltd.com
    Web site: chapelleltd.com

STERLING and the distinctive Sterling logo are registered trademarks of Sterling Publishing Co., Inc.

Library of Congress Cataloging-in-Publication Data

Hiney, Mary Jo.
  Quilted bags & purses / Mary Jo Hiney.
    p. cm.
  Includes index.
  ISBN 1-4027-0201-9
1. Handbags. 2. Patchwork--Patterns. 3. Appliqued--Patterns.
4. Quilting. I. Title.

TT667.H56 2005
646.4'8--dc22   2004030352

10 9 8 7 6 5 4 3 2 1

Published by Sterling Publishing Co., Inc.
387 Park Avenue South, New York, NY 10016
©2005 by Mary Jo Hiney
Distributed in Canada by Sterling Publishing
c/o Manda Group, 165 Dufferin Street
Toronto, Ontario, Canada M6K 3H6
Distributed in the United Kingdom by GMC Distribution Services
Castle Place, 166 High Street, Lewes, East Sussex, England BN7 1XU
Distributed in Australia by Capricorn Link (Australia) Pty. Ltd.
P.O. Box 704, Windsor, NSW 2756, Australia

Printed in China
All Rights Reserved

Sterling ISBN-13: 978-1-4027-0201-3 (hardcover)
      ISBN-10: 1-4027-0201-9

Sterling ISBN-13: 978-1-4027-5390-9 (paperback)
      ISBN-10: 1-4027-5390-X

For information about custom editions, special sales, premium and corporate purchases, please contact Sterling Special Sales Department at 800-805-5489 or specialsales@sterlingpublishing.com.

table of contents

A systematic arrangement of data for ready reference. A list of topics following in a book.

introduction

A part of a book preliminary to the main portion that announces, explains, or sets something in proper perspective.

So many handbags, so little time. Bags and purses are fun to create, have, own, or give and they are very useful. A handbag can add just the right touch to an outfit; but it can also be the perfect accompaniment to a chair back. Making a purse is an enjoyable process, from deciding upon which to make, to shopping for fabulous fabrics and embellishments, to creating and finishing your chosen purse. An added plus is the little-known fact that creating a handbag from start to finish is a good source for improving your self-worth, because will be so proud to purse your new creation!

Have you noticed that when choosing a new purse, one is very interested in checking out the organizational compartments within? Have you ever thought about how those little compartments are made? You will enjoy learning the proper sequence to creating compartments. You might invent some new ones, too. Just about every purse in this book has some sort of compartment internally or externally to help you with that initial curiosity and subsequent organizational needs.

What about closures? Have you noticed how you wished a bag had a zipper, especially when that bag falls upside down in the backseat of your car and the entire contents roll around on the car floor for the rest of time? Hmmm, . . . zippers are looking pretty important, aren't they? Not to worry; these purses have zippers and they have magnetic closures and they have flaps with buttons and some have all three at the same time.

The bags and purses in this book have been created in small, medium, and large sizes. Some use fabrics with a fashion-oriented appeal and others use fabrics with home decor in mind. There is variety in types, shapes, closures, compartments, and handles. There is variety in quilt-related techniques, embellishments, and fabrics. And there is variety in personality. Each purse has a quality reflecting a positive emotion through color, pattern, or shape. Each purse asks that we consider a state of mind: one that may reflect your individuality or that of a friend; one that encourages or uplifts; one that represents a hope or a goal; one that brings a smile. Your biggest challenge will be in deciding with which to start and to whom you will give your first purse.

I hope you will enjoy making the bags and purses presented in this book, because I so enjoyed creating them with all of our needs in mind.

femininity & charm on page 36

general instructions

An outline or manual of procedures that is applicable to, or affecting the whole.

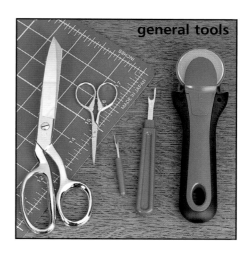

general tools

general tools

Following are notions and tools to have on hand before beginning purses, along with the required fabrics and notions for each project.

- Circle template
- Cotton swab
- Fray preventative
- Grid-lined ruler
- Iron/ironing board
- Photocopier
- Quilter's ruler
- Quilting pins
- Rotary cutter (shown above right)
- Scissors: craft; fabric (shown above right)
- Seam ripper (shown above right)
- Self-healing cutting mat (shown above right)
- Sewing machine
- Sewing-machine needles
- Spray starch
- Straight pins
- Tape measure
- Tracing paper
- Water-soluble fabric-marking pen
- Zipper foot attachment for sewing machine

getting ready

Read through the instructions for the purse you are planning to make. Approach making a purse in increments, setting yourself up for success. Before starting to make the purse, you will need to:

a. Shop for the items on the materials list. Check your private stash for basics, especially notions and tools.

b. Photocopy the patterns required, enlarging them if necessary.

c. Preshrink the fabric if you plan to launder the purse. Some fabrics are designed to present an aged or vintage appearance after being laundered, which can create a terrific look.

d. Cut out the fabrics, using the necessary patterns and/or measurements.

e. Cut with accuracy. Whenever possible, use a rotary cutter, quilter's ruler, and self-healing cutting mat to cut accurately straight purse pieces. Use the cutting mat and rotary cutter to trim purse pieces to size within the assembly process.

f. Make certain to mark the fabric pieces with all construction details prior to sewing. When assembling the purses, refer to the pattern pieces for additional information.

g. Dig in and have fun! Do not be afraid of sewing the little tiny zipper. Just think of how many things will remain in your upside-down purse because you braved "the" zipper. Go a little crazy and get a zipper in a fun shade.

basic design elements

appliqué, freezer-paper technique:

Note: If necessary, make certain to enlarge pattern to required percentage on photocopier.

1. Trace or photocopy the appliqué pattern onto paper. Cut out paper pattern.

2. Reverse and trace appliqué pattern onto matte side of the freezer paper.

3. Press shiny side of freezer-paper face downward onto wrong side of appliqué fabric.

4. Cut fabric applique, leaving a ¼" seam allowance all around freezer paper pattern. Spray a bit of spray starch into a small container. Saturate cotton swab with spray starch. Dab outer edge of fabric with swab. Clip outer edge of fabric up to freezer paper.

5. Using iron, steam-press outer edges of fabric up over edge of freezer paper, being careful to maintain appliqués shape.

6. Remove freezer paper and press again.

7. Using doubled thread, hand-appliqué the outer edge of appliqué in place.

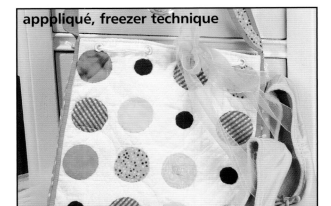

appplidqué, freezer technique

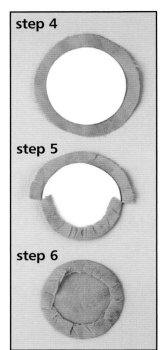

step 4

step 5

step 6

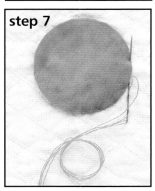

step 7

applique, raw-edge technique:

Note: If necessary, make certain to enlarge pattern to required percentage on photocopier.

1. Trace or photocopy the appliqué pattern onto paper. Cut out paper pattern.

2. Spray-starch area of fabric that is slightly larger than appliqué pattern piece. Reverse and trace appliqué pattern backward onto wrong side of fabric. Cut out piece on traced line.

3. Dab light touches of tacky glue onto wrong side of fabric appliqué. Position, then lightly press in place, using iron.

4. Three choices for securing appliqué to fabric:

   • Cover entire appliqué design with ivory bridal illusion or tulle. Using free-motion technique, machine-sew around each piece.

   • Machine-sew a narrow zigzag, buttonhole, or blind-hem stitch around each appliqué piece in a design, spacing stitches fairly closely together

   • Machine-satin-stitch around each appliqué piece in design, spacing the stitches very tightly together.

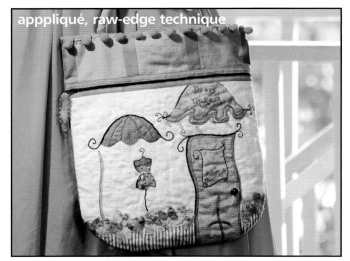

appplidqué, raw-edge technique

beading:

1. Use doubled thread to stitch beads in place on a purse front. Several different needle types can be used for this task. The obvious choice is the beading needle and for some beads, it is the only needle that will slide through a bead hole. Other needle choices include a very fine embroidery needle and a milliner's needle. Try either as a needle option.

beading

2. To begin beading in a knotless fashion, slip both thread ends through the needle eye, having the looped thread end as the longer length. Stitch into purse at necessary location, or entry point, and slip needle through thread loop before pulling thread taut, thus knotting the thread on the top of the fabric without a knot. Slip needle through beads and position beads at thread entry point. Stitch back into fabric at opposite end of bead, then stitch thread through the fabric and back to the original entry point, double-stitching beads in place. Using same thread, slide several more beads onto needle. Move beads to meet previous set and stitch back into fabric at opposite end of beads, as before.

foundation piecing:

Foundation fabrics must be stable enough to stitch fabric pieces onto, and sheer enough to see through. The best example of a foundation fabric is lightweight nonwoven interfacing that is nonfusible. Purchase the very lightest weight you can find. Using a fine-tipped permanent ink fabric marker, trace directly onto the interfacing. As the interfacing is very lightweight, it adds little bulk to a foundation-pieced quilt block or project and eliminates the

foundation piecing

need to tear away foundation-piecing paper. It is a bit of a nuisance to trace onto the nonwoven interfacing, but not nearly as much of an ordeal as tearing paper away from a sewn block. Other examples of foundation fabrics are muslin, paper, and tear-away backing. A non-tear-away foundation fabric will add an extra piece of fabric to quilt through. You may wish to experiment to discover your preferred foundation material.

Foundation piecing often requires preseaming. Preseaming means that two pieces of fabric may need to be stitched together before being stitched onto the foundation. The fabrics must be cut to the shape of the area and sewn together. They are then treated as one unit, with the seam resting on the appropriate seam line. Except when preseaming is required, fabric pieces need not be cut perfectly. Use strips, rectangles, squares, or any other odd-shaped scrap material.

Make certain fabric is at least ⅜" larger on all sides than the area it is to cover. As triangular shapes are more difficult to piece, use generously sized fabric pieces and position pieces carefully on the foundation. Some fabric is wasted in foundation piecing, but the time saved is well worth the results. Through practice, you will discover the most effective and least wasteful sizes to cut fabric pieces.

foundation piecing instructions:

Note: If necessary, make certain to enlarge pattern to required percentage on photocopier.

1. Transfer the pattern onto foundation. Using a fine-tipped permanent ink fabric marker or #2 pencil, write all numbers on foundation.

step 1

2. Cut fabric piece for block. When making many blocks, make a chart as an aid to note fabrics, number placements, cut sizes, and quantities needed for each fabric.

3. Turn over foundation with unmarked side up. Place fabric piece 1, right side up, on shape 1. If foundation is not sheer, hold foundation up to a light source to make certain that fabric overlaps at least ¼" on all sides of shape 1. Pin, glue, or hold in place.

4. Make certain that fabric piece 2 overlaps at least ¼" on all sides of shape 2. Place fabric piece 2 on fabric piece 1, right sides together.

5. Turn over foundation, with marked side up. Sew along line between shapes 1 and 2, using a very small stitch. *Note: This is helpful if paper has been used as the foundation.* Begin and end two or three stitches beyond the line.

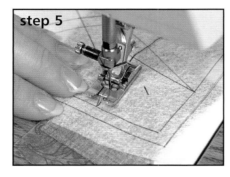
step 5

6. Trim excess fabric ⅛"–¼" past seam line. Take care not to cut foundation.

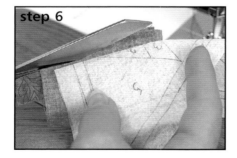
step 6

7. Turn over foundation, with the unmarked side up. Open fabric piece 2 and finger-press seam. Pin or glue in place, if necessary.

8. Make certain that fabric piece 3 overlaps at least ¼" on all sides of shape 3. Place fabric piece 3 on fabric piece 1, with right sides together. Secure in place. Repeat Steps 5–6.

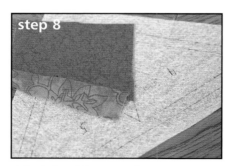
step 8

9. Press once all pieces have been sewn in place on a unit. Stitch ⅛" inward from outer edge of foundation's seam allowance. Trim the foundation unit on seam line. Assemble units as directed.

free-motion machine quilting:

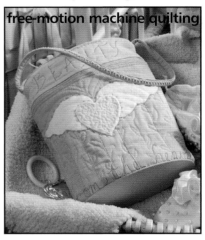
free-motion machine quilting

- For machine quilting, replace presser foot with a darning foot. Refer to the sewing machine manufacturer's directions for proper installation of the darning foot, etc. Lower the feed dogs. With purse piece in place under darning foot, begin sewing, moving the purse piece around in a random or planned design.

- Free-motion machine quilting is done on layered purse pieces (those with backing/batting/top layers or batting/top layers).

- Purse pieces will shrink in size during the quilting process, so make certain to allow ½" extra around each piece prior to quilting, then trim to the appropriate pattern size once the quilting is completed.

piecework:

piecework

The traditional method of piecing, whereby individual pieces with seam allowances are cut out and then sewn together in the pieced design. Many of the pieced designs for the purses have been done using the foundation-piecing method, although each design can be accomplished using the traditional method as well. If you prefer to work a design in the traditional method, create patterns for the piecework, then add a ¼" seam allowance all around each pattern.

floss and ribbon stitches:

backstitch

1. Bring needle up at A; go down at B, one opening to the left. Come up at C. Go down at D.

bullion lazy daisy

1. Bring needle up at A. Keep ribbon flat, untwisted and full. Go down through fabric at B and up through at C, but do not pull through. Snugly wrap ribbon around needle tip one to three times. Holding finger over wrapped ribbon, pull needle through ribbon and down through fabric.

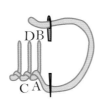

2. Repeat as necessary.

buttonhole

1. Bring needle up at A; go down at B. Come up again at C, keeping thread under needle. Go down at D.

2. Repeat, making all stitches equal.

couching

1. Complete a straight stitch base by coming up at A and down at B. Make certain ribbon is flat and loose.

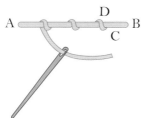

2. Make a short, tight stitch across ribbon base to "couch" straight stitch. Come up at C on one side of ribbon. Go down at D on opposite side of ribbon. This will cause the ribbon to gather and pucker.

3. Repeat as necessary.

french knot

1. Bring needle up at A. Loosely wrap floss once around needle. Go down at B, one opening across from A. Pull floss taut as needle is pushed down through fabric. Carry floss across back of work between knots.

2. Repeat as necessary.

lazy daisy

1. Bring needle up at A, keeping floss/ribbon flat, untwisted and full. Go down at A, pulling flat.

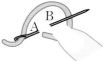

2. Come up at B, keeping floss under needle to form a loop. Pull floss/ribbon through, leaving loose loop full. To hold loop in place, go down at C, one opening across from B, forming a long stitch over loop.

3. Repeat as necessary.

outline

1. Bring needle up at A, keeping floss to the right and above the needle. Push needle down at B. Come back up at C.

2. Repeat as necessary.

ribbon

1. Bring needle up at A. Lay ribbon flat on fabric. At end of stitch, pierce ribbon with the needle. Slowly pull length of ribbon through back, allowing ribbon ends to curl.

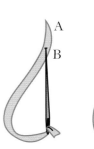

2. Repeat as necessary.

floss and ribbon stitches

basic construction elements

applying zippers for closures or pockets:

1. If it is necessary to begin with a zipper that is longer in length than the opening requires, mark length zipper needs to be based on zipper opening or instructions. Using doubled thread, stitch across zipper coils several times on mark to create new length for zipper. Trim away excess zipper ⅛" past new end. *Note: For some purses and bags, the longer-length zipper is trimmed once it has been sewn where designated.*

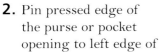
zippers

2. Pin pressed edge of the purse or pocket opening to left edge of zipper tape, aligning pressed fabric edge to edge of zipper coil, beginning and ending zipper where designated in purse instructions. Using a zipper foot, machine-sew pressed edge of purse or pocket opening to zipper tape. Align and sew opposite pressed edge of purse or pocket opening to opposite side of zipper tape in same manner.

3. Finish as indicated in purse instructions.

backing:

For those purse pieces that are machine-quilted, generally lining fabric is used as the backing layer. However, for some purses, a generic fabric is used and the purse has an additional lining fabric.

batting and fleece options:

Batting is used as the middle layer for the purse pieces, whether or not the purse pieces have been quilted. For some of the purses, pieces have been machine-quilted with the batting layer but without the backing layer. Bonded cotton batting or fusible fleece is the preferred batting to use for the purses. Both are interchangeable in regard to purse assembly and I suggest you choose the one that you prefer once you've had a chance to work with both of them. When possible, trim the batting away from the seam line in order to cut down seam line bulk.

edge-pressing:

Edge-pressing is a preliminary pressing step that exposes the seam line when turned right side out. It is used when it is not possible to press a seam allowance open. Unlike pressing a seam allowance open, in this case, only one side of the seam allowance has been pressed open. To do this, fold over the top layer of a seam allowance and press.

interfacings:

- Nonwoven lightweight interfacing is the best example of a foundation fabric to use when foundation-piecing.

- Fusible woven interfacing is used to add body and sturdiness to fabric. It helps in creating a shapely purse, but still makes sewing easy.

- Knit, fusible interfacing is used when fabric needs a little more body without becoming stiff.

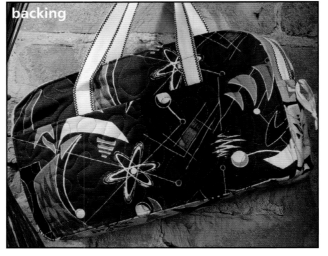

backing

pressing:

Pressing is a key factor in purse assembly. Besides using the traditional iron and ironing board, a sleeve board can be helpful for pressing small, hard to reach areas. A spray bottle with water helps in achieving a crisply pressed seam. Always test a scrap of fabric for heat resistance prior to pressing. If too hot, an iron can melt and/or scorch fibers. A presscloth is a handy helper as well when pressing.

small purses

A bag or tote having comparatively little size or dimensions. Relative to size determined by capacity.

celebration

To observe a notable holiday with festivities.

finished size
• 8" x 8½", side gusset 1½"

cotton fabrics
Brown (1 variation)
• Brown broadcloth (¼ yd) for inner zippered pocket underlay; circle appliqués

Olive green (2 variations)
• 44"-wide light olive polka-dot (¼ yd) for Pattern B; Pattern E
• 44"-wide olive/gold striped (¼ yd) for Pattern D; circle appliqués

Pink (4 variations)
• 44"-wide dark pink variegated (⅛ yd) for handle bottom; binding; circle appliqués
• 44"-wide pink variegated (⅛ yd) for Pattern C; Pattern B lining; circle appliqués
• 44"-wide pink polka-dot (⅛ yd) for handle top; circle appliqués
• Light pink tone-on-tone (2" sq.) for circle appliqué

White (1 variation)
• 44"–60"-wide white textured (¼ yd) for Pattern A

embellishments
• ⅛"-wide white soutache (1¼ yd)
• 8mm x 10mm pink butterfly bead

notions
• ³⁄₁₆" white eyelet (10)
• 7" white nylon zippers (2)
• 44"-wide cotton batting (⅜ yd)
• Matching threads

tools
• General Tools on page 5
• Eyelet tool
• Hand-sewing needle
• Large safety pin
• Quilter's freezer paper

cutting tote fabrics
Note: Enlarge Celebration Patterns on pages 16–18 200% unless otherwise indicated.

1. Using Pattern A, cut one front and one back ½" larger all around than pattern (to be trimmed to pattern size after quilting step) from white textured cotton. Using water-soluble fabric-marking pen, transfer the circle appliqué placement marks onto the front, (16 for the front). Transfer circle appliqué placement mark onto the back in the same manner (one for the back). Cut one front and one back ½" larger all around than pattern from cotton batting. Cut one front and one back from brown cotton broadcloth for inner zippered pocket underlay.

2. Using Pattern B, cut one side gusset on fold line from light olive polka-dot cotton ½" larger all around than pattern (to be trimmed to pattern size after quilting step). Cut one from cotton batting ½" larger all around than pattern. Cut one from pink variegated cotton for lining B.

3. Using Pattern C, cut two upper zippered pocket pieces from pink variegated cotton.

4. Using Pattern D, cut two lower zippered pocket pieces from olive/gold striped cotton.

5. Using Pattern E, cut two small inside pockets from light olive polka-dot cotton.

6. Cut two 2" x 26" strips from dark pink variegated cotton for bindings.

Continued on page 14.

Continued from page 12.

7. Cut one 1" x 24" strip from pink polka-dot cotton for handle top.

8. Cut one 2" x 26" strip from dark pink variegated cotton for handle bottom.

9. Cut two 1¼" x 3" strips from olive/gold striped cotton for zippered pocket end strips.

10. Using water-soluble fabric-marking pen, mark all fabric pieces as indicated on all the patterns assembly markings. Refer to pattern pieces when assembling each purse.

creating appliquéd front and back

1. For front circle appliqués, cut 2" circles from the following fabrics: dark pink variegated (3); pink variegated (2); pink polka-dot (2); olive/gold striped (4).

2. Cut four 1¼" circles from the brown broadcloth.

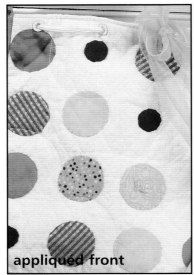

appliqued front

3. For back circle appliqués, cut one 4" circle from pink variegated and one 2½" circle from dark pink variegated.

Freezer paper appliqué technique:

4. Cut one 1½" circle and one ¾" circle from the freezer paper.

5. Press shiny side of freezer paper face downward onto wrong side of one 2" dark pink variegated circle. Spray some starch into lid or small container. Saturate cotton swab with spray starch. Dab outer edge of fabric with swab. Clip outer edge of fabric up to freezer paper. Using steam iron, press outer edges of fabric up over edge of freezer paper, being careful to maintain the circular shape. Remove freezer paper and press again.

6. Using needle and doubled thread, hand-appliqué outer edge of circle to front. Refer to photo on page 13 for color placement. Repeat for each 1½" and ¾" circle appliqués for front.

7. Cut one 3½" circle and one 2" circle from freezer paper. Follow Steps 5–6 for two largest circles. Hand-appliqué larger circle in place on back. Hand-appliqué smaller circle centered over large circle.

quilting front, back, and side gusset

1. Place wrong side of front against front batting piece. Using water-soluble marking pen, trace five 3" circles onto front in a diagonal pattern. Machine-quilt through two layers on drawn circles. Mist quilted front with water-filled spray bottle, press dry. Repeat to quilt back in the same manner. Stitch ⅜" inward from the outer edges on both front and back pieces.

side gusset binding

2. Place wrong side of side gusset against side gusset batting piece. Free-motion machine-quilt piece through the two layers.

3. Pin Pattern A to quilted front. Trim to pattern size. Repeat for back. Pin Pattern B to quilted side gusset. Trim to pattern size.

assembling purse

Note: All seam allowances are ½" unless otherwise indicated.

Sew front to side gusset:

1. With wrong sides facing, pin side gusset to front, matching center bottom and curved corner dots. Clip side gusset close to seam line at curved corner dots. With side gusset piece up, sew side gusset to front. Machine-sew ⅛" inward from seam line. Trim seam allowance just past second row of stitching.

Sew binding to front seam/side gusset technique:

2. Press 2" x 26" dark pink variegated strip in half, matching long edges. Working from front, pin and sew binding to side gusset/front seam line,

using a ¼" seam allowance. Sew again ⅛" inward from seam line. Trim seam allowance just past second row of stitching. Press binding toward seam allowance. Fold binding over and around to other side of seam. Stitch finished edge of binding to seam line on side gusset side.

3. Repeat Steps 1–2 on page 14 and above for the back/side gusset.

making handle

Note: For a more sturdy handle, fuse medium-weight interfacing to the handle pieces prior to beginning.

1. Working with top and bottom handle pieces, machine-sew handle top to handle bottom, aligning one long edge, using a ¼" seam allowance. Press seam allowance toward handle bottom piece. Align remaining long edges of handle top and bottom. Sew long edges together, using a ¼" seam allowance, forming a tube. Press seam allowance toward handle bottom piece.

handle

2. Pin large safety pin to one layer of tube at an end. Close safety pin and slip it within the tube. Push safety pin through tube, adjusting fabric as it goes through and out other end, turning tube right side out. Evenly adjust seams along side edges and press. Pin handle ends to upper edges of side gusset, right sides facing. Baste-stitch ends to side gusset, using a ⅜" seam allowance.

making zippered pocket

1. Measure 6½" from top stop of zipper. Using needle and doubled thread, stitch across zipper coils several times on mark to create a new, shorter length for zipper. Trim away excess zipper ½" past new end.

2. Working with upper and lower zippered pocket pieces, press fabric edge (for zipper placement) under ½" to fabric wrong side. Working between the dots for zipper placement, pin pressed edge of

upper pocket to left edge of zipper tape, aligning fabric edge to edge of zipper coil, beginning and ending zipper at dots. Using a zipper foot, machine-sew upper pocket pressed edge to zipper tape. Align and sew lower pocket pressed edge to opposite side of zipper tape in the same manner.

3. Press long edges of 1¼" x 3" olive/gold strip under ¼" to wrong side. Sew one short end of strip to end of zipper and upper/lower pocket pieces, with right sides facing, using a ¼" seam allowance with strip. Fold strip over to extend past end of pocket pieces. Topstitch along top, inner edge, and bottom of strip through all layers. Repeat for other end of zipper, making a clean and sturdy finish for zippered pocket. Repeat for second pocket.

making small inside pocket

1. Fold small inside pocket in half on fold line, right sides facing. Sew pocket side edges together, using a ¼" seam allowance. Clip bulk from corners. Edge-press seam allowance open. Turn pocket right side out. Press flat. Repeat for the second pocket.

2. Sew small inside pocket to bottom half of zippered pocket where indicated on pattern.

assembling lining

1. Layer front inner zippered pocket underlay piece with one zippered pocket, wrong sides facing. Repeat for other pieces.

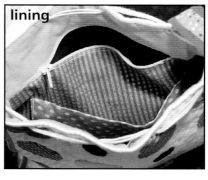

lining

2. Pin and sew side gusset lining to layered pocket front, right sides facing, using a ½" seam allowance. Match center bottom and curved corner dots. Clip side gusset close to seam line at curved corner dots. Sew again ⅛" from first seam line. Trim away excess seam allowance just past second row of stitching. Press seam allowance toward side gusset. Topstitch just inside seam line. Repeat for back.

finishing

1. Slip lining over tote, right sides facing, aligning upper edges. Sew around upper edges, using a ½" seam allowance and leaving a 3" opening on back when sewing. Trim seam allowance to ¼". Press seam allowance toward lining. Turn right side out through opening. Slip lining into tote and press along top edges. Topstitch close to seam line, stitching opening closed in the process.

2. Mark top edge for eyelet placement: Mark 1" inward on front and back from both side edges, ⅜" down from top edge. Mark 2" inward from these side marks. On side gusset, mark ¼" inward from top side edges. Using eyelet tool and referring to manufacturer's directions, apply an eyelet at each mark.

3. Cut soutache in half. Slip one length in and out of eyelets, beginning and ending on the same side of side gusset. Repeat with other length of soutache, beginning and ending with opposite side of side gusset.

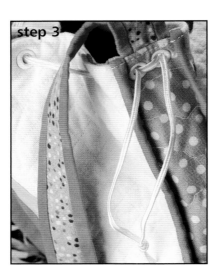

4. Tie soutache ends into a knot. Coat ends with fray preventative. When dry, trim ends at a slant. Pull on both cords to close tote.

5. Stitch the butterfly bead to the palest pink appliquéd circle.

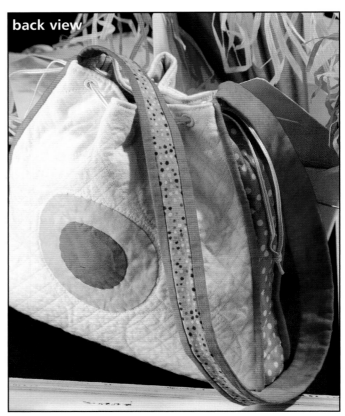

back view

celebration pattern

Enlarge pattern on this page 200%.

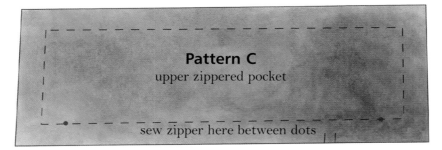

Pattern C
upper zippered pocket

sew zipper here between dots

celebration patterns

Enlarge patterns on this page 200%.

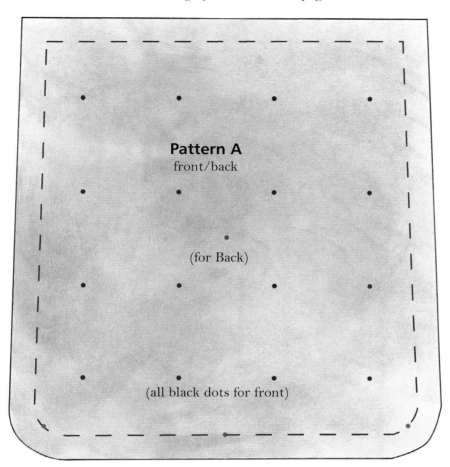

Pattern A
front/back

(for Back)

(all black dots for front)

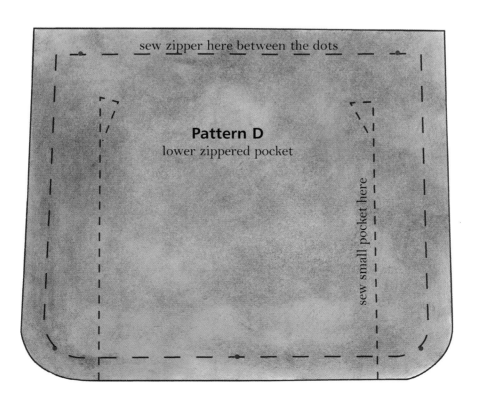

sew zipper here between the dots

Pattern D
lower zippered pocket

sew small pocket here

celebration patterns

Enlarge patterns on this page 200%.

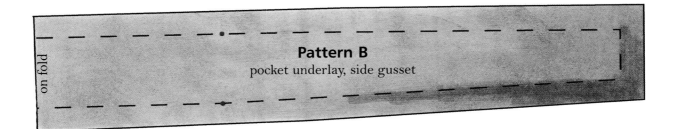

Pattern B
pocket underlay, side gusset

on fold

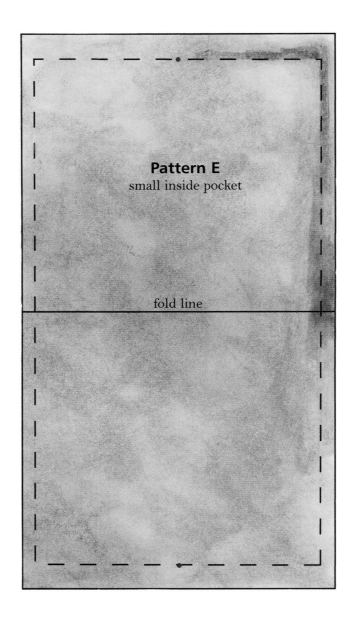

Pattern E
small inside pocket

fold line

cheerfulness

Full of good spirits. Likely to dispel gloom or worry.

Cheerfulness photo shown on page 22

finished size
• 8" x 9¾"

cotton fabrics
Aqua (13 variations)
• 44"-wide aqua flower print (⅜ yd) for Pattern A
• Twelve different prints, light to dark color range, assorted styles (3" x 9" each) for yo-yos

Orange (12 variations)
• Nine different bright orange (3" x 6" each) for yo-yos
• Three different light orange prints (3" x 6" each) for yo-yos

Pink (9 variations)
• Six different bright pink (3" x 6" each) for yo-yos
• Three different light pink prints (3" x 6" each) for yo-yos

White (2 variations)
• 44"-wide white floral print (¼ yd) for Pattern B
• 44"-wide white small floral print (⅜ yd) for Pattern C; Pattern A

Yellow (12 variations)
• Nine different bright orange (3" x 6" each) for yo-yos
• Three different light orange prints (3" x 6" each) for yo-yos

embellishments
• 15" sq. vintage print hanky
• 7mm-wide orange silk ribbon (2 yds)

• 6mm silver round beads (28)
• 8mm light green round glass beads (4)
• 8mm turquoise round glass beads (4)
• 10mm turquoise round glass beads (4)
• 10mm x 30mm aqua cloisonné tube-shaped beads (2)
• 12mm aqua cloisonné round beads (4)
• 12mm x 18mm aqua ceramic oval-shaped beads (12)

notions
• 7" white nylon zippers (2)
• 18-gauge copper wire (30")
• Matching threads

tools
• General Tools on page 5
• Needle-nosed pliers
• Needles: embroidery size 1; hand-sewing;
• Wire cutters

cutting tote fabrics

Note: Enlarge Cheerfulness Patterns on page 23 200% unless otherwise indicated.

1. Using Pattern A, cut one front underlay and one back from aqua floral print fabric. Cut two pocket underlays from white small floral print fabric.

2. Using Pattern B, cut two upper zippered pockets from white floral print fabric. Cut one 1¼" x 10" strip.

3. Using Pattern C, cut two lower zippered pockets from white small floral print fabric.

4. Using water-soluble fabric-marking pen, mark all fabric pieces as indicated with the pattern's assembly markings. Refer to pattern pieces when assembling each purse.

creating front

1. For yo-yos, cut 2½" circles from the following fabrics: aqua variations (36 altogether); bright orange variations (19 altogether); light orange variations (3 altogether); bright pink variations (15 altogether); light pink variations (3 altogether); bright yellow variations (19 altogether); light yellow variations (3 altogether).

2. Hand-stitch each circle into a yo-yo, following Yo-yo technique below.

Yo-yo technique:

3. Using needle and doubled thread, knot ends together. With fabric circle wrong side up, fold a scant ⅛" edge of circle to wrong side while gather-stitching along folded edge. (See Illus. A)

Illus. A

4. Pull on thread so that gathered edge cups to center. (See Illus. B) Secure gathers by knotting thread. (See Illus. C)

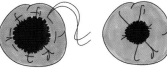

Illus. B   Illus. C

Making Grandmother's Flower Garden Design:

5. Refer to Color Placement diagram below to make Grandmother's Flower Garden Design with yo-yos for front. Begin with pink, bottom-center flower:

a. With gathered center sides facing, stitch a bright pink yo-yo to a light pink yo-yo (See Illus. D), taking three small stitches. Stitch a bright pink yo-yo to other edge of light pink yo-yo.

Illus. D

b. Stitch two bright pink yo-yos to right edge of center yo-yos. Stitch two bright pink yo-yos to left edge of center. (See Illus. E)

Illus. E

c. Stitch aqua yo-yos around bright pink yo-yos. (See Illus. F)

Illus. F

6. Continue to stitch yo-yos together. (See Illus. G)

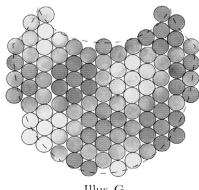

Illus. G

assembling purse

Note: All pieces have ½" seam allowance unless otherwise indicated.

1. Position assembled yo-yo front piece onto front underlay fabric. Stitch centers of yo-yos to front underlay, keeping stitches 1" away from outer edge of front underlay. Pin the outer edge yo-yos away from the seam line.

2. Pin a corner of print hanky centered onto top half of back. Trim hanky to back shape along upper edges. Stitch hemmed edge of hanky to back.

3. Machine-baste hanky to back along upper edges.

4. Pin and sew front to back, right sides facing, along side and lower curved edges. Press seam allowance open. Turn right side out.

5. Replace pinned-out-of-the-way yo-yos so they overlap onto side and lower-edge seam and slightly onto the back. Hand-stitch edges of outer yo-yos in place.

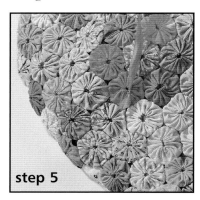

step 5

making zippered pocket

1. Working with upper and lower zippered pocket pieces, press the fabric edge (for zipper placement) under ½" to fabric wrong side. Working between dots for zipper placement, pin pressed edge of upper pocket to left edge of zipper tape, aligning fabric edge to edge of zipper coil, beginning and ending zipper at dots. Using a zipper foot, machine-sew upper pocket pressed edge to zipper tape. Align and sew lower pocket pressed edge to opposite side of zipper tape in the same manner.

2. Press long edges of 1¼" x 10" white floral print under ¼" to wrong side. Sew one short end of strip to end of zipper and upper/lower pocket pieces, with right sides facing, using a ¼" seam allowance with the strip. Fold strip over to extend past end of pocket pieces. Topstitch along top, inner edge, and bottom of the strip through all layers. Repeat for the other end of the zipper, making a clean and sturdy finish for the zippered pocket. Repeat for the second pocket.

assembling lining

1. Layer pocket underlay piece with one zippered pocket, wrong sides facing. Machine-baste along outer edges. Repeat for other pieces.

2. Place two lay-ered zippered pockets with zippered sides facing. Sew along side and lower curved edges, begin-ning with a ½" seam allowance, but increasing seam allowance to ⅜" just past first stitches, leaving a 3" opening along one side edge. Taper stitches at opposite end back to ½" seam allowance. Sew again ⅛" inward from seam line. Trim seam allowance just past second row of stitching. Press seam allowance toward one side.

lining

finishing

1. Slip lining over purse, right sides facing, align-ing upper edges. Sew around the upper edges, using a ½" seam allow-ance. Trim bulk away from upper tips. Trim remaining seam allow-ance to ¼". Clip curves to seam line. Press seam allowance toward lining. Turn right side out through lining opening. Push out tips. Slip lining into purse and press along top edges.

back view

making handle

1. Using wire cut-ters, cut wire in half, creating two 15" lengths. Working with one length, coil one end three times around tip of needle-nosed pliers.

handle

2. Slip beads onto wire as desired. Trim wire ¾" past last bead, then coil the end three times around tip of needle-nosed pliers. Repeat with the second wire length.

3. Cut an 18" length from 7mm ribbon. Slip the ribbon end through embroidery needle and knot onto needle as for ribbon embroidery. Knot the opposite end.

4. Working with tote front, slip ribbon up through inside of one tip from lining seam opening. Securely stitch ribbon through coiled end of one handle and onto the tip of tote several times so that handle is securely fastened to tote tip. Do not cut ribbon. Stitch ribbon in and out of front upper edge, making stitches ½" apart, ending stitches at center of front.

5. Repeat Step 2 with other end of beaded handle.

6. Pull gently on two ribbon ends so that upper edge of front gathers slightly. Tie ribbon ends together into a knot. Trim each end at a slant and knot each above cut.

7. Cut a 24" length from the 7mm ribbon. Repeat Step 2 for purse back, continuing ribbon along to opposite upper tip. Securely stitch other end of handle to tip with the ribbon. Trim the excess ribbon.

cheerfulness patterns

Enlarge patterns on this page 400% unless otherwise as indicated.

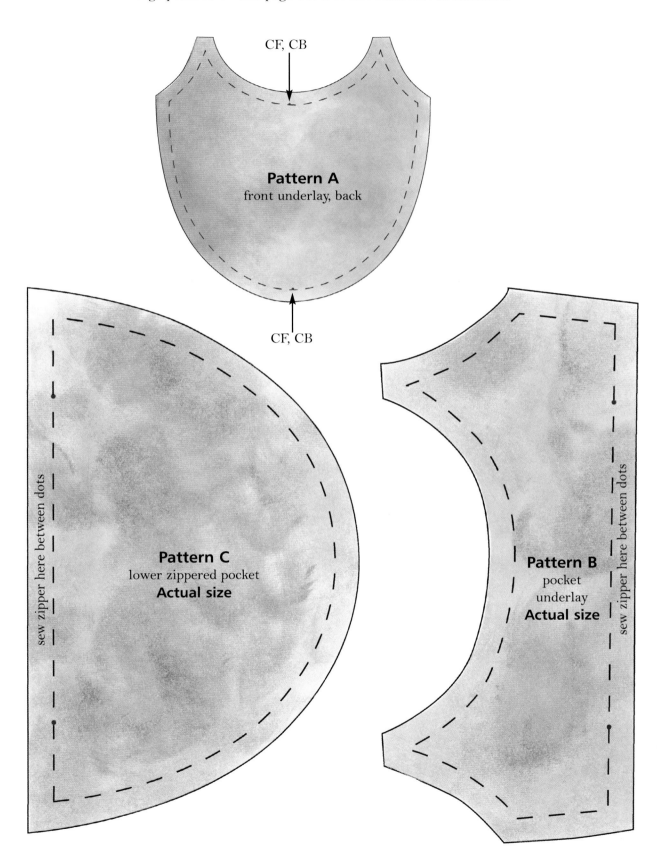

CF, CB

Pattern A
front underlay, back

CF, CB

sew zipper here between dots

Pattern C
lower zippered pocket
Actual size

sew zipper here between dots

Pattern B
pocket
underlay
Actual size

freedom

The quality or state of being free. The liberation from the power of another.

finished size
- 6½" (tapered top) x 8" (bottom) x 8"

fabrics
- 44"-wide muslin (⅛ yd)

Brown silk dupioni (1 variation)
- Medium brown (¼ yd) for Piecing Pattern #3 for back, Appliqué Patterns #3, 12, 14

Green silk dupioni (3 variations)
- Chartreuse (6" x 11") for Piecing Pattern #5; Appliqués Patterns #5, #13; circle E
- Light olive (6" x 11") for Piecing Pattern #1; Appliqué Patterns #1, #18; circle B
- Seafoam (6" x 7") for Appliqués Patterns #2, #11, #19; circles C, D

Pink silk dupioni (2 variations)
- Coral (6" x 7") for Appliqué Patterns #4, #8
- Light pink (⅛ yd) for Pattern A for Front, Piecing Pattern #2

Purple silk dupioni (2 variations)
- Fuchsia (⅛ yd) for Piecing Pattern #4, Appliqué Pattern #6, #17; circle A; Pattern A for Front/Back lining; inner pocket piece; Pattern B for purse bottom, lining, Handle
- Orchid (6" x 11") for Piecing Pattern #6, Appliqué Patterns #7, #9, #16

Rust silk dupioni (1 variation)
- Rust (6" x 7") Appliqué Patterns #10, #15; circles C, D

notions
- ⅛"-wide white cord (½ yd)
- ¾" magnetic purse bag closure
- 22"-wide medium-weight woven fusible interfacing (¾ yd)
- 44"-wide cotton batting (⅛ yd)
- Matching threads

tools
- General Tools on page 5
- Hand-sewing needle
- Large safety pin
- Masking tape
- Quilter's freezer paper
- Translucent tape

cutting fabrics for front appliquéd design
Note: Enlarge Freedom Patterns on pages 28–31 200% unless otherwise indicated.

1. Using Pattern A, cut one front ½" larger all around than pattern (to be trimmed to pattern size after quilting step) from pink dupioni and fusible interfacing. *Note: The pink dupioni front piece is used as the base fabric. The appliqué pieces are applied to the base, leaving two spaces of the design open to reveal the base fabric.*

2. Fuse interfacing to wrong side of pink dupioni front.

3. Trim Appliqué Patterns #1–#19 for front pieces close to outer edges, then tape each to dull side of freezer paper. Cut appliqué pieces from freezer paper, using craft scissors.

4. Press shiny side of freezer paper face downward onto wrong side of silk fabrics, using the following pieces on fabrics listed below:
   - Chartreuse–#5, #13, 2" circle E
   - Coral–#4, #8
   - Fuchsia–#6, #17, 1¼" circle A
   - Light olive–#1, #18, 1" circle B
   - Medium brown–#3, #12, #14
   - Orchid–#7, #9, #16
   - Rust–#10, #15
   - Seafoam–#2, #11, #19

5. For seamed circles: Cut one piece each from rust and seafoam fabrics 1¼" x 4". Machine-sew pieces along 4" edges, right sides facing, using ¼" seam allowance. Press.

Continued on page 26.

Continued from page 24.

seam allowance open. Press shiny side of freezer-paper ¾" circle C and 1½" circle D onto fabric wrong side, aligning center of circles on fabric seam line.

6. The edges of each freezer-paper piece may have an outer seam allowance, an underlap allowance, and/or an appliquéd edge. An outer seam allowance is indicated with ⅜" seam allowance. An underlap allowance is with a "U" along the pattern edge. The applique edge is indicated with dots along the pattern edge. For edges with outer seam allowance, trim fabric ⅜" larger than size of freezer-paper piece at that edge. *Note: This will allow for shrinkage when the appliquéd design is quilted.* For edges with underlap allowance, trim fabric exactly to size of freezer-paper piece at that edge. For appliquéd (finished) edges and circles, trim fabric with a ¼" fabric allowance past the freezer-paper edge.

7. Using water-soluble fabric-marking pen, mark all fabric pieces as indicated with the patterns assembly markings. Refer to pattern pieces when assembling each purse.

appliquéing front design

1. Spray some starch into lid or small container. Saturate cotton swab with spray starch. Dab outer edge of fabric to be appliquéd with swab. Clip outer edge of fabric up to freezer paper. Using iron on steam, press outer edges of fabric up over edge of freezer paper, being careful to maintain the edge's shape. Remove freezer paper and press again.

2. Work design by section. (See Illus. A) *Note: The design has been separated into sections that are numbered 1–6.*

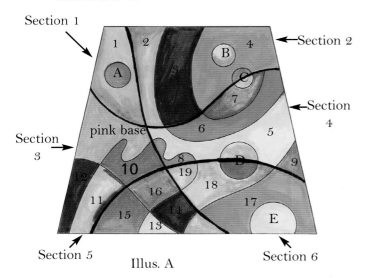

Section 1
Section 2
Section 4
Section 3
pink base
Section 5
Illus. A
Section 6

3. Within each section are numbered pieces. The pieces are applied to base fabric in numerical order. Working with section 1, pin piece #1 in place. Working with section 2, position piece #2, overlapping finished edge onto underlap edge of #1. Pin in place. Position pieces #3 and #4 in the same manner. Working with section 4, position and pin pieces #5–#9. Continue in this manner, working section 3, then #5 and #6. Piece #19 is finished along all edges.

4. Using needle and doubled thread, hand-appliqué each finished edge to each underlap edge and through to base fabric. Appliqué circles in place.

cutting and piecing purse back

1. Cut one Piecing Pattern #1 on pages 29–30 for back from light olive. Cut one Piecing Pattern #2 for back from light pink. Cut one Piecing Pattern #3 for back from medium brown. Cut one Piecing Pattern #4 for back from fuchsia. Cut one Piecing Pattern #5 for back from chartreuse. Cut one Piecing Pattern #6 for back from orchid.

2. Piece back, using a ¼" seam allowances. Machine-sew #1 and #2 together along adjacent edge, clipping curves as necessary to seam line. Press seam allowance toward olive. Sew #3 and #4 together along adjacent edges. Press seam allowance toward fuchsia. Sew #5 and #6 together along adjacent edges. Press seam allowance toward chartreuse. Sew #1/#2 to #3/#4, matching seam lines. Clip inner curving edges to seam line before stitching. Press seam allowance toward #3/#4. Sew four pieces to #5/#6, matching seam lines and clipping inner curving edges to seam line before stitching. Press seam allowance toward #5/#6.

machine-quilting front and back

1. Using Pattern A, cut one front and back ½" larger all around than pattern from muslin and batting.

2. Layer muslin, batting, and front together, wrong sides facing. Layer muslin, batting and back together, wrong sides facing.

3. Machine-quilt front with an all over small meandering stitch. Quilt around the circle appliqués. Machine-quilt the back so that seam lines are "echoed."

4. Using Pattern A, trim quilted front and back to pattern size.

5. Sew front to back along side edges, using a ½" seam allowance. Press seam allowance open. Pin and machine-baste upper edges of front/back under ½" to fabric wrong side.

cutting remaining purse fabric pieces

1. Cut a piece of fabric 2½" x 28" for handle from fuchsia dupioni.

2. Using Pattern A, cut one front and back for lining from fuchsia and fusible interfacing.

3. Using Pattern A, cut two inner pockets along fold from fuchsia where indicated on pattern.

4. Using Pattern B, cut purse bottom and bottom lining from fuchsia. Cut one purse bottom from fusible interfacing.

making handle

1. Press both long edges of handle piece under ½" to fabric wrong side. Press piece in half, aligning long edges.

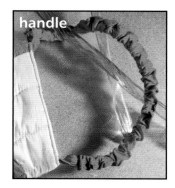

2. Sew the handle together along pressed-under edges through all layers.

3. Wrap tape around cord at end and 14" from end. Cut cord through middle of tape. Using safety pin attached to one cord end, slip cord through handle. Hand-stitch cord to handle 1½" from entry end, wrapping and cinching thread around handle to secure cord in place. *Note: This will create a flat end to the handle.*

4. Extend cord through handle to opposite end. *Note: The handle fabric will ruche over the cord.* Wrap and cinch thread around handle 1½" from end to secure cord in place, as was done with the opposite end, creating again a flat end.

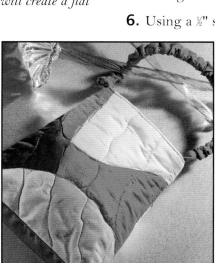

back view

5. Pin flat ends of handle to purse turned-under upper edges at side seams, working with a ½" seam allowance. Stitch handle ends in place at side seams, while folding raw ends of handle to inside top edge of purse.

making pockets and lining

1. Fuse the interfacing to wrong side of the front and back lining pieces.

lining

2. Press each pocket in half along fold line. Position pockets on front and back lining pieces, aligning bottom edges. Pin and machine-sew the pocket to front lining along vertical center.

3. Pin and sew front to back lining pieces along side edges through all layers, right sides facing. Press seam allowance open.

finishing

1. Pin and machine-baste upper edges of front/back lining under ½" to fabric wrong side.

2. Apply magnetic closure to upper edges of front/back lining, following manufacturer's directions, placing pieces ½" down from turned-under edges.

3. Slip lining into purse, with wrong sides facing, aligning the upper edges. Sew lining to purse.

4. Topstitch purse upper edge. Turn inside out. Align and pin together bottom edges of purse and lining.

5. Fuse interfacing to wrong side of purse bottom. Layer purse bottom with purse bottom lining wrong sides facing.

6. Using a ½" seam allowance, sew purse bottom to bottom edges of purse/lining, right sides facing, matching center the front and back dots, corner Xs and side seam dots.

7. Sew again ⅛" from stitch line. Trim seam allowance close to second line of stitching.

8. Overcast trimmed seam allowance.

9. Turn right side out and press bottom-edge seam line.

freedom patterns
Enlarge patterns on this page 200%.

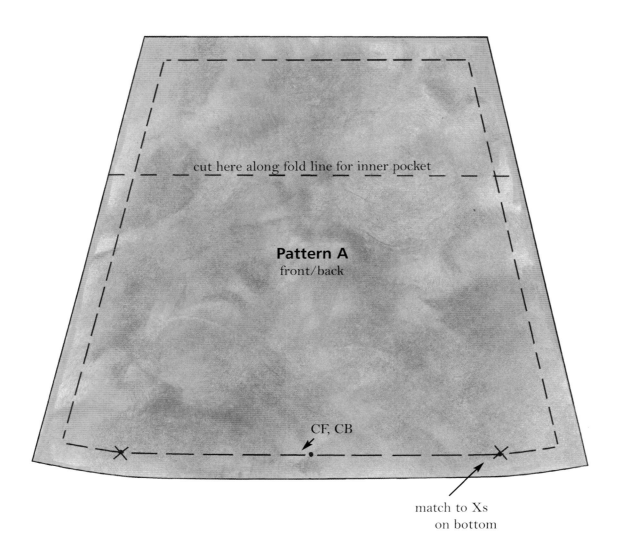

cut here along fold line for inner pocket

Pattern A
front/back

CF, CB

match to Xs
on bottom

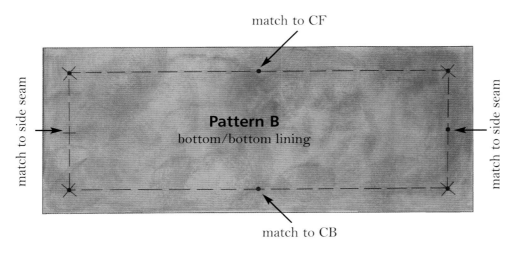

match to CF

match to side seam

Pattern B
bottom/bottom lining

match to side seam

match to CB

freedom patterns

Enlarge patterns on this page 200%.

Piecing
Pattern #1

Piecing
Pattern #3

Piecing
Pattern #2

Piecing
Pattern #5

Piecing Pattern #4

freedom patterns

Enlarge patterns on this page 200%.

Note: Dots along pattern edge indicate the edge is appliqued. "U" along pattern edge indicates the edge is underlapped.

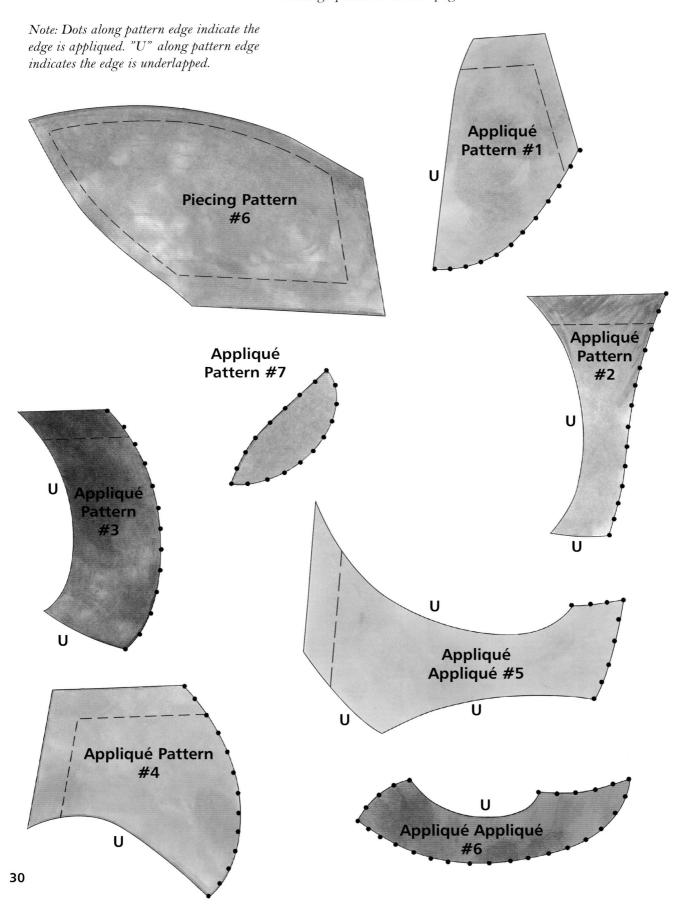

Appliqué Pattern #1

Piecing Pattern #6

Appliqué Pattern #2

Appliqué Pattern #7

Appliqué Pattern #3

Appliqué Appliqué #5

Appliqué Pattern #4

Appliqué Appliqué #6

freedom patterns

Enlarge patterns on this page 200%.

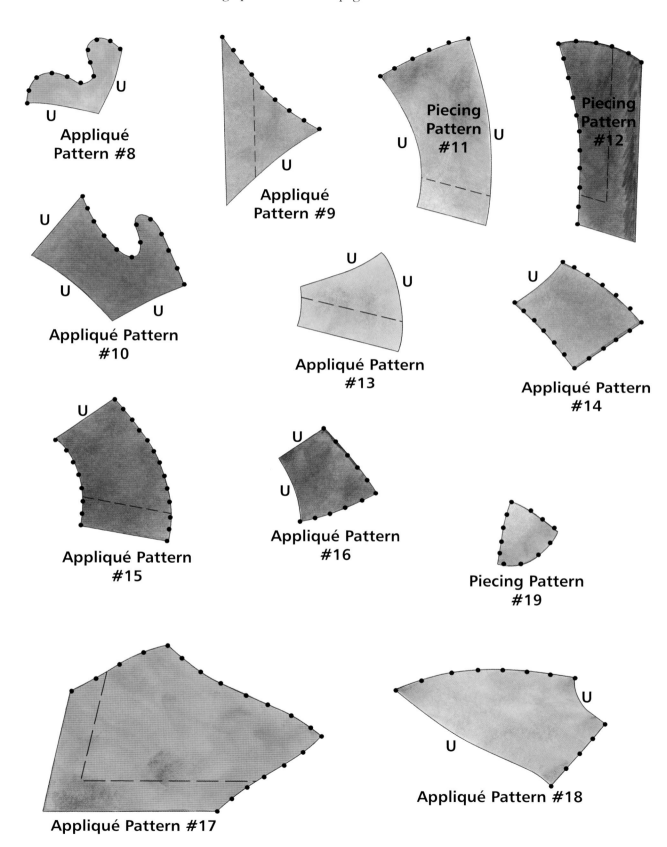

Appliqué Pattern #8

Appliqué Pattern #9

Piecing Pattern #11

Piecing Pattern #12

Appliqué Pattern #10

Appliqué Pattern #13

Appliqué Pattern #14

Appliqué Pattern #15

Appliqué Pattern #16

Piecing Pattern #19

Appliqué Pattern #17

Appliqué Pattern #18

truthfulness

Sincerity in action, character, and utterance.

finished size
- 10" x 7" x 2"

embellishments
- 3½" x 5" bamboo handle
- 4"-long brown tassel

fabrics

Brown (3 variations)
- 44"-wide bronze imitation aged leather (¼ yd) for top and bottom strip B; inner pocket D
- 44"-wide dark purple-brown silk dupioni (½ yd) for quilt block; spine/back A; inside lining C; zipper strip E; handle
- Medium brown silk dupioni (6" x 11") for quilt block

Gold (1 variation)
- Rich gold silk dupioni (6" x 7") for quilt block

Olive Green (1 variation)
- Dark olive silk dupioni (6" x 7") for quilt block

Purple (1 variation)
- Muted plum silk dupioni (6" x 7") for quilt block

Rust (2 variations)
- Rich rust silk dupioni (6" x 7") for quilt block
- Salmon silk dupioni (6" x 7") for quilt block

notions
- 22"-wide lightweight nonwoven interfacing (¼ yd) for quilt block
- 22"-wide medium-weight fusible woven interfacing (½ yd) for spine/back A; inside lining C
- 24" dark brown zipper
- Matching threads

tools
- General Tools on page 5
- Fine-tipped black permanent ink fabric-marking pen
- Hand-sewing needle

making foundation-pieced quilt block

Note: Enlarge Truthfulness Patterns on page 35 200% unless otherwise indicated.

Refer to Foundation Piecing on pages 7–8 before beginning.

1. Using Unit A Pattern for foundation-pieced quilt block, trace four left- and four right-facing Unit As onto lightweight nonwoven interfacing, using permanent ink pen and grid-lined ruler. Be certain to add the seam allowance to each traced piece.

2. Trace four of Unit B Pattern onto lightweight nonwoven interfacing in the same manner as Step 1.

3. For Unit A, cut rectangles or squares from silk dupioni fabrics that are ⅜" larger all around than the area the piece will be sewn to. Use the medium brown for spaces #1, #4, and #6. Use the dark purple-brown for spaces #2, #3, #5, and #6a. *Note: The pieces #6 and #6a are preseamed before sewing in place on the foundation.* Use the dark olive for space #7.

4. Foundation-piece four left- and four right-facing Unit As. Sew each left- and right-facing Unit A together. Press seam allowances open.

5. For Unit B, cut rectangles in the same manner as in Step 3. Use dark olive green for space #1. Use muted plum for spaces #2, and #3. Use rich gold for space #4. Use rich rust for space #5. Use salmon for space #6.

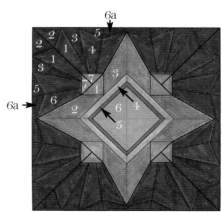

Illus. A

Continued on page 34.

Continued from page 32.

6. Sew a Unit B to each assembled Unit A. (See Illus. A)

7. Sew four assembled units together to make quilt block. Trim outer seam allowance so block measures 7" square.

cutting fabrics

1. Cut 10½" x 7" piece one for spine/back from dark purple-brown dupioni and fusible woven interfacing. Cut 3" x 8" piece for handle from dark purple-brown dupioni. Cut one 17" x 10" for inside lining from dark purple-brown dupioni and fusible woven interfacing.

2. Using Pattern E, cut two zipper strips from dark purple-brown dupioni and cut one from the fusible woven interfacing. Cut two 3" x 8" for handle piece from dark purple-brown dupioni and woven, fusible interfacing.

3. Cut two 17" x 2¼" for top and bottom strips from bronze imitation aged leather.

4. Cut two 10½" x 8" inner pockets from bronze imitation aged leather.

sewing outer purse pieces together

1. Fuse interfacing to wrong side of spine/back A piece. Sew one short edge of the spine/back A to quilt block, right sides facing, using a ¼" seam allowance. Press seam allowance toward spine/back A.

2. Machine-sew top and bottom strips B to the top and bottom of the quilt block/spine/back piece, right sides facing, using a ¼" seam allowance. Direct seam allowance toward imitation leather.

3. Topstitch close to the seam line on imitation leather pieces. Do not press the imitation leather.

4. Measure and mark 7¼" from both short edges of assembled piece, using water-soluble fabric-marking pen. Fold piece on one mark and topstitch close to folded edge. Repeat with the remaining mark. *Note: These topstitched lines designate the spine for the purse.*

making inside pockets

1. Fold under one long edge of each inner pocket D 1¼" to wrong side. Stitch inner edge to form pocket hem.

2. Fuse interfacing to wrong side of inside lining C.

3. Position remaining long edge of each pocket over right and left sides of the lining, placing wrong side of pockets against right side of lining. Pin in place.

4. Pin together lining with pockets and assembled outer pieces, wrong sides facing.

making zippered side

1. Cut interfacing piece for the zipper strips E in half lengthwise. Fuse each half to one side of the zipper strips E on the wrong side of the fabric.

2. Press strips in half, wrong sides facing.

3. Pin folded edges to the zipper, aligning fabric edge to edge of zipper coil. Using a zipper foot on sewing machine, sew folded edges to zipper tape. Machine-sew again a scant ¼" from first row of stitching. *Note: The zipper will be a bit longer than the strips. The excess zipper will be trimmed once the zippered strip has been sewn to the purse.*

sewing zippered side to purse top, side, and bottom

1. Working with purse front with quilt block, sew one long edge of zippered strip to top, sides and bottom of front, with right sides facing, using a ½" seam allowance. Match dots from zipper strip E pattern to outer and inner corners of purse front, sewing through all layers.

2. Sew opposite long edge of zippered strip to top, sides, and bottom of back in same manner as Step 1 above. Sew top and bottom ends of strip to spine section of the purse, using ½" seam allowance.

3. Sew again ⅛" from first row of stitching. Trim seam allowance close to second stitched row. Overcast seam allowance. Press seam allowance toward strip. Attach tassel to zipper.

tassel

making handle piece

1. Fuse the interfacing to wrong side of handle piece. Fold piece in half, matching short edges with the right sides facing. Sew the short edges, leaving a 1" opening in the seam line. Press seam allowance open.

handle

2. Position seam line centered between longer edges, with right sides facing. Sew longer edges, using a ¼" seam allowance. Turn handle piece right side out through seam opening. Press.

3. Place handle piece centered over spine on outside of purse. Sew one long edge of handle piece to spine. Slip handle under handle piece. Sew the remaining long edge of handle piece to spine, securing the handle in place.

truthfulness patterns

Enlarge patterns as indicated.

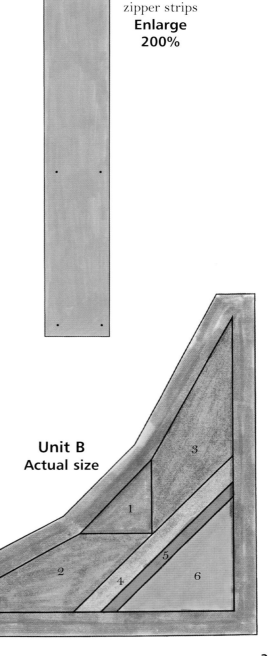

Pattern E
zipper strips
Enlarge 200%

Unit A
Actual size

make one left and one right

2
1
3
4
5
6
6a

Unit B
Actual size

3
1
2
5
4
6

femininity & charm

The quality or nature of the female sex that allures, fascinates, or attracts.

finished size
• 9" x 9½"

cotton fabric
• 44"–54"-wide muted seafoam floral matelassé (⅝ yd)

embellishments
• ½"-wide mauve chiffon rosebud trim (⅝ yd)
• 1"-wide ecru pleated tricot trim (⅓ yd)
• 1"-wide pale seafoam grosgrain ribbon (½ yd)
• 5" yellow/rose silk flower
• 11/0 silver triangle-cut seed beads
• 14/0 metallic burgundy seed beads
• 6mm ivory pearl beads (3)
• Vintage butterfly brooch

notions
• ¾" magnetic tote-bag closure
• Matching thread

tools
• General Tools on page 5
• Needles: beading; hand-sewing

cutting tote fabrics

Note: Enlarge Femininity & Charm Patterns on pages 39–40 200% unless otherwise indicated.

1. Using Pattern A, cut two left- and two-right facing fronts from cotton matelassé fabric.

2. Using Pattern B, cut two backs from the cotton matelassé fabric.

3. Using Pattern C, cut one pocket from the cotton matelassé fabric.

4. Cut one bottom binding strip 2" x 8½" from cotton matelassé fabric. Cut one handle strip 2" x 20" from cotton matelassé fabric.

5. Using water-soluble fabric-marking pen, mark all fabric pieces as indicated on all the patterns assembly markings. Refer to pattern pieces when assembling each tote.

sewing overlapping fronts

1. Machine-baste pleated trim to right side of one left-facing front, along diagonal edge, tapering trim at left and right edges. Place trim-basted front with a second front, right sides facing. Sew diagonal edge, catching in trim when sewing. Trim seam allowance to ¼" and press it toward outer side.

2. Place remaining front pieces with right sides facing. Sew diagonal edge and trim seam allowance to ¼". Press seam allowance toward outer side.

3. Overlap trimmed front onto remaining front, having trimmed front on top, creating cross-wrapped appearance.

4. Cut two ⅛" long slits into the inside of the underlapping front at the center, making slits ½" downward from the upper edge.

Continued on page 38.

Continued from page 36.

5. Push prongs from one part of the magnetic snap through slits, working from right side of inside front. Working from underside of inside front, slip the "washer" over prongs. Flatten prongs outward over washer. Pin together overlapping fronts along top-placed front diagonal edges.

6. Lift upper layer of top-placed front. Using water-soluble fabric-marking pen, draw a line on inside of bottom layer along vertical center of front.

beading

7. With upper layer still lifted out of way, sew along vertical center line through remaining three layers, making certain to not stitch through magnetic closure when sewing. Replace the upper layer. *Note: This step has created two small pockets, one that is on the outside of the purse and another on the inside of the tote.*

8. Pin front layers together along side edges.

sewing back

1. Hem back pocket. Turn upper edge under ¼". Turn under again along fold line. Sew along turned-under edge. Press under side edges. Position back pocket on one back by aligning pocket bottom edge with back bottom edge, centering pocket between side edges. Sew pocket in place along side edges. Machine-baste across bottom edges.

2. Place backs with right sides facing. Sew curved edge. Trim seam allowance to ¼" and press toward outer side.

sewing front to back

1. Lift inside layer of back away from outside layer of back. Pin and sew outside layer of back to front along side edges, right sides facing. Trim seam allowance, using a grading method. To grade:

a. Trim underneath seam allowance layer to ¼". Trim middle seam allowance layers to ⅜".

b. Press seam allowances toward back.

2. Replace inside layer of the back. Turn under side edges and hand-stitch in place along side seams, enclosing side seams.

3. Apply magnetic closure to inside center of back where fronts cross at center. Cut two ⅛" long slits into inside back where magnetic closure on front lines up to back. Push prongs from other half of magnetic closure through slits. Slip washer over prongs from underside of back. Flatten prongs.

beading front

1. Using beading needle and matching thread, accent some of floral design on the fabric with beading, making certain to keep front layers separated when beading. Work beading by alternating silver and burgundy seed beads.

2. To bead, bring needle to surface at an entry point. Slide four beads onto needle, alternating bead shades. Move beads to entry point and extend them on fabric.

3. Stitch back into fabric at end of beads and back up at original entry point.

4. Slip needle back through the four beads, then slide another four alternating beads onto the needle. *Note: This method double-stitches the beads in place.*

5. Extend beads on fabric as before and stitch into fabric at end of beads. Stitch back up into fabric where second group of beads began; slip needle through second group of beads, then slide another four alternating beads onto needle.

6. Continue to bead front in this manner, using as many beads as desired.

7. Stitch pearls where desired on front.

making handle

1. Press two long handle edges under ½" to wrong side. Press in half, aligning the pressed-under edges. Machine-sew along both long edges.

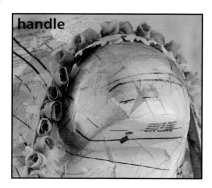

handle

2. Position handle ends at upper edge of side seams, turning handle ends under. Hand-stitch the handle ends to the side seams.

3. Stitch rosebud trim over handle.

finishing

1. Bind bottom edge of tote with binding strip.

2. Hand-stitch upper edge of grosgrain ribbon around tote bottom, placing grosgrain lower edge ¼" up from finished edge.

3. Stitch vintage brooch and silk flower to front.

femininity & charm pattern

Enlarge pattern on this page 200%.

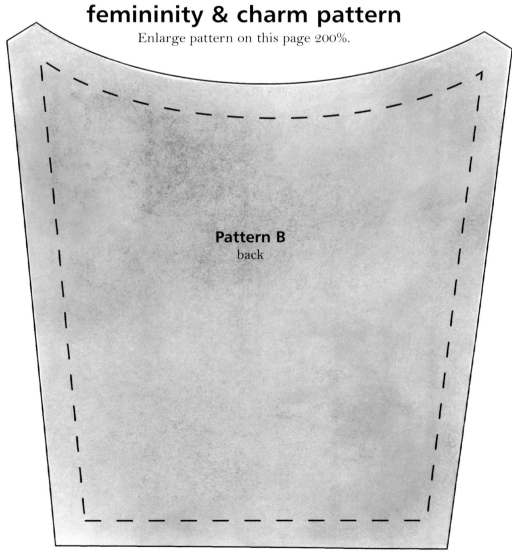

Pattern B
back

femininity & charm patterns

Enlarge patterns on this page 200%.

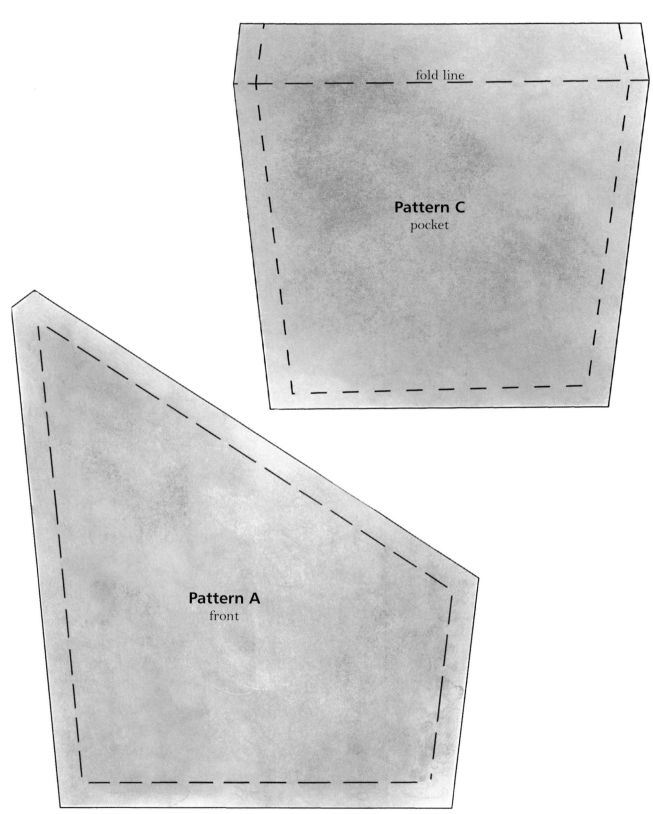

fold line

Pattern C
pocket

Pattern A
front

constancy

A steadfastness of mind under duress. Freedom from change.

Constancy photo shown on page 44

finished size
• 7½" x 4"

cotton fabrics

Gray (1 variation)
• Gray/tan batik (4" x 12") for foundation piecing

Green (5 variations)
• 44"-wide leaf green batik for (¼ yd) C; E backing; foundation piecing
• 44"-wide teal patterned (⅛ yd) for Pattern B; foundation piecing
• Green/blue batik (4" x 12") for foundation piecing
• Hunter green batik (4" x 12") for foundation piecing
• Olive batik (4" x 12") for foundation piecing

Royal blue (3 variations)
• 44"-wide royal blue/black batik (¼ yd) for Pattern D; foundation piecing
• 44"-wide royal blue/turquoise batik (⅛ yd) for Pattern A; zipper pull F; strip G; foundation piecing
• Royal blue/white patterned (4" x 12") for foundation piecing

notions
• 22"-wide lightweight nonwoven interfacing for foundation piecing (¼ yd)
• 22"-wide lightweight fusible woven interfacing for Pattern A; Pattern C; Pattern D (½ yd)
• Fusible fleece (9" x 10") for Pattern E
• Matching threads
• Olive green zippers: 7"; 18"

tools
• General Tools on page 5
• Fine-tipped brown permanent ink fabric-marking pen
• Hand-sewing needle

cutting fabrics

Note: Enlarge Constancy Patterns on pages 45–46 200% unless otherwise indicated.

1. Using Pattern A, cut two for inside zippered pocket from the royal blue/turquoise batik. Cut one from the fusible interfacing.

2. Using Pattern B, cut four for inner side gusset from teal patterned fabric.

3. Using Pattern C, cut two for inner binding from leaf green batik. Cut one from fusible interfacing.

4. Using Pattern D, cut two for inner flat pocket from royal blue/black batik. Cut one from fusible interfacing.

5. Using Pattern E, cut one each for outer binding backing from leaf green batik and fusible interfacing. Cut one from fusible fleece that does not have the ¼" seam allowance added.

6. Cut one zipper pull F piece 13" x 1¼" from royal blue/turquoise batik.

7. Cut one assembly strip G piece 8¼" x 1⅜" from royal blue/turquoise batik.

8. Using water-soluble fabric-marking pen, mark all fabric pieces as indicated with the patterns assembly markings. Refer to pattern pieces when assembling each purse.

making inside zippered pocket

1. Fuse interfacing to wrong side of one inside zippered pocket A piece.

2. Place two inside zippered pockets with right sides facing.

3. Machine-sew rectangular space for zipper where indicated on pattern. (See Illus. A)

Illus. A

4. Cut through center of rectangular space and clip to the corners. (See Illus. B) Edge-press the seam allowance open. Turn right side out. Press.

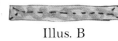

Illus. B

5. Position the 7" zipper centered underneath opening. Machine-sew the zipper to the opening along the inner edges of the opening. (See Illus. C) Trim away excess zipper ¼" past opening.

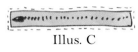

Illus. C

6. Press longer edges of pocket under ¼" to wrong side (side with excess zipper visible).

7. Fold pocket in half along zipper fold line, with wrong sides facing. Trim piece along side edges so it measures 7" in width.

8. Sew longer edges together close to pressed-under edges. Sew side edges together, using a ⅛" seam allowance. (See Illus. D)

Illus. D

sewing inner side gussets to inside zippered pocket

1. Place two inner side gusset pieces with right sides facing. Sew top and bottom curved edges, using a ¼" seam allowance. Edge-press seam allowance open. Turn right side out and press flat.

2. Repeat Step 1 for other inner side gusset pieces.

3. Fold one inner side gusset in half along fold line indicated on pattern. Press.

4. Slip left end of inside zippered pocket into pressed crease on inner side gusset, aligning top edges. Sew gusset to pocket along side edges, using a ⅛" seam allowance.

5. Repeat Step 4 for other inner side gusset piece. (See Illus. E)

Illus. E

6. Accordion-pleat inner side gusset pieces where indicated on pattern. Press. (See Illus. F)

Illus. F

making inner binding and inner flat pocket

1. Fuse interfacing to wrong side of one inner binding C piece.

2. Place inner binding C pieces with right sides facing. Sew around outer edges, using a ¼" seam allowance, leaving opening along one edge in order to turn piece right side out.

3. Clip curves. Turn right side out. Press flat.

4. Fuse interfacing to wrong side of one inner flat pocket D piece.

5. Place two inner flat pocket D pieces with right sides facing. Sew longer edges (top and bottom), using a ¼" seam allowance. Edge-press seam allowances open. Turn right side out. Press flat.

6. Place inner flat pocket onto inner binding where indicated on pattern. Sew inner flat pocket to inner binding along stitch lines. (See Illus. G) Wrap and pin excess side seam allowance from inner flat pocket around to back side of inner binding.

Illus. G

7. Wrap excess side seam allowance from one inner side gusset around to back side of inner binding, positioning upper edge from gusset with upper edge of inner pocket. Topstitch inner side gusset to pocket and binding along the side edge. (See Illus. H)

Illus. H

8. Repeat Step 7 for opposite side of binding, working with second inner side gusset.

9. Repeat Steps 7–8 for other half of pocket and binding. *Note: This step is a bit awkward, as the binding will need to close somewhat in order to attach the gussets.*

10. Hand-stitch one half of inner binding to wrong side of 18" zipper near edge of zipper tape. Begin approximately 1" past zipper top stop and end approximately 1" past end stop. *Note: The excess zipper will wrap underneath the inner binding.* (See Illus. I)

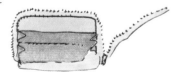

Illus. I

11. Repeat Step 10 for opposite half of inner binding. Wrap excess zipper to underside of inner binding.

foundation-piecing outer binding

Refer to Foundation Piecing on pages 7–8 before beginning.

1. Using Unit A Pattern on page 46 for foundation pieced quilt block, trace four unit As onto lightweight nonwoven interfacing, using permanent ink pen and grid-lined ruler.

2. Cut rectangles or squares from nine cotton fabrics for foundation piecing that are ⅜" larger all around than area the piece will be sewn to.

3. Foundation-piece four unit As, alternating fabric positions on four units.

4. Machine-sew two unit As together along one long edge. Press seam allowance open.

5. Repeat Step 4 for the remaining two Unit A pieces.

6. Sew assembly strip G piece between two unit A sets, forming outer binding. Press seam allowances open.

7. Fuse fleece to wrong side of outer binding. Fuse interfacing to wrong side of outer binding E piece.

8. Place foundation-pieced outer binding with interfaced outer binding with right sides facing. Sew pieces together along outer edges, using a ¼" seam allowance and leaving opening along one side. Clip curves. Edge press seam allowance open.

9. Turn right side out through opening. Slipstitch opening closed.

10. Wrap outer binding around inner binding. Pin in place.

foundation-piecing outer binding

11. Pin and stitch one half of outer binding to right side of zipper near edge of zipper tape, as was done with Step 10 for making inner binding and inner flat pocket on page 42.

12. Repeat Step 9 for opposite half of the outer binding.

13. Working with zipper pull F piece, press long edges under ¼" to wrong side. Press in half, aligning the pressed-under edges. Sew the layers together along pressed-under edges.

14. Slip zipper pull fabric piece through zipper pull. Sew layers together. Coat ends with fray preventative. When dry, cut ends at a slant.

inside view

constancy patterns

Enlarge patterns on this page 200%.

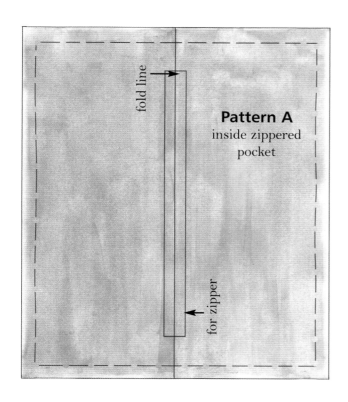

Pattern A
inside zippered pocket

fold line

for zipper

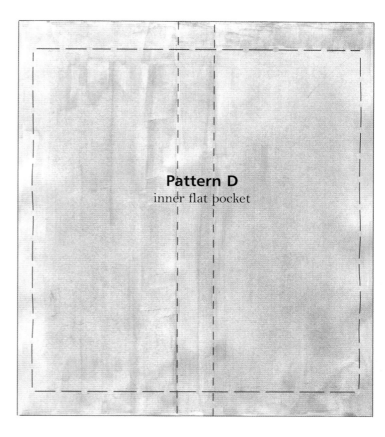

Pattern D
inner flat pocket

Pattern B
inner side gusset
Actual size

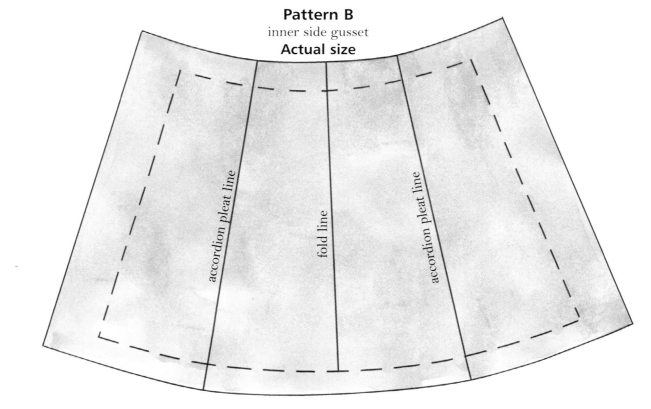

accordion pleat line

fold line

accordion pleat line

constancy patterns

Enlarge patterns on this page 200%.

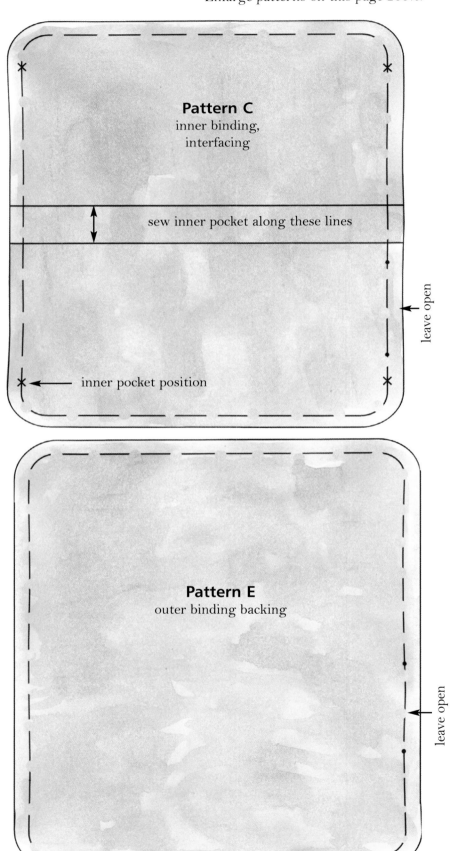

Pattern C
inner binding,
interfacing

sew inner pocket along these lines

leave open

inner pocket position

Pattern E
outer binding backing

leave open

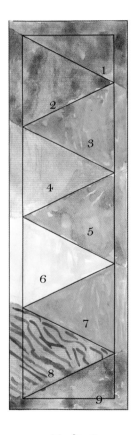

Unit A

clarity

The quality or state of being luminous and clear. Free from obscurity or ambiguity.

Clarity photo shown on page 48

finished size
• 8" x 9", side gusset 1¾"

cotton fabrics
Gold (2 variations)
• Curry gold patterned (3½ x 1") for quilt block Unit B
• Tan/gold variegated (3" sq.) for quilt block unit B

Green (2 variations)
• Hunter green variegated (1½" sq.) for quilt block Unit B
• Olive patterned (3" x 1") for quilt block Unit B

Purple (3 variations)
• 44"-wide plum speckled (⅛ yd) for side gusset C; binding E
• Dark plum patterned (4½" x 9") for quilt block Units A, B
• Purple batik (6" x 12") for Pattern A; side gusset C lining

Rust (6 variations)
• 44"-wide rust/plum striped (¼ yd) for sashing B; back D
• 44"-wide rust swirl (¼ yd) for front/back lining D
• Four different rust prints (3" x 6" each) for quilt block Unit A

embellishments
• ¼"-wide white cord (½ yd)
• ½"-wide gold-edged purple ribbon (1½ yd)
• ¾" dia. brown leather button

notions
• 22"-wide lightweight fusible woven interfacing (½ yd) for Pattern A; side gusset C; back; D lining
• 22"-wide lightweight nonwoven interfacing (¼ yd) for foundation-pieced quilt block
• Matching threads

tools
• General Tools on page 5
• Fine-tipped brown permanent ink
• Hand-sewing needle
• Masking tape

making foundation-pieced quilt block

Refer to Foundation Piecing on pages 7–8 before beginning.

1. Using Unit A Pattern on page 51 for foundation-pieced quilt block, trace one left- and one right-facing Unit A onto lightweight nonwoven interfacing, using the permanent ink pen and grid-lined ruler. Be certain to add the seam allowance to each traced piece.

2. Trace one Unit B Pattern on page 51 onto lightweight nonwoven interfacing in the same manner as in Step 1.

3. For unit A, cut rectangles or squares from cotton fabrics that are ⅜" larger all around than area the piece will be sewn to. Use four rust prints for spaces #1, #3, and #5. Use dark plum patterned fabric for spaces #2, #4, and #6.

4. Foundation-piece the left- and right-facing unit As. Machine-sew left- and right-facing unit As together. Press seam allowance open.

Continued on page 49.

Continued from page 47.

5. For unit B, cut rectangles or squares in the same manner as in Step 3 on page 47. Use hunter green for space #1. Use the dark plum patterned fabric for spaces #2, #3, #7, #8, #11, #12, #15, and #16. Use curry gold patterned fabric for space #4.

Use light olive patterned fabric for space #5. Use tan/gold variegated fabric for space #6. Use four rust prints for spaces #9, #10, #13, and #14.

6. Sew unit B to assembled unit A. (See Illus. A) Press seam allowance open.

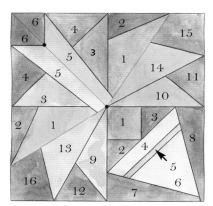

Illus. A

cutting fabrics

1. Using Clarity Pattern A on page 51, cut four corner triangles from purple batik. Cut four from fusible interfacing.

2. Cut four 6¼" x 1" strips from rust/plum striped for sashing B.

3. Cut one 24" x 2¼" piece for side gusset C each from plum speckled, purple batik, and fusible interfacing.

4. Cut one 8⅜" square from rust/plum striped for back D, two 8⅜" squares from rust swirl for front/back lining D. Cut two 8⅜" squares from fusible interfacing for front/back D lining.

5. Cut one 18½" x 2¾" strip each from plum speckled and fusible interfacing for binding strip E.

6. Using water-soluble fabric-marking pen, mark all fabric pieces as indicated on all the patterns assembly markings. Refer to pattern pieces when assembling each purse.

sewing outer purse pieces together

1. Sew sashing B strips to four sides of quilt block, using a ¼" seam allowance. Press seam allowance toward sashing.

2. Fuse interfacing to corner triangles on fabric wrong side.

3. To complete purse front, sew diagonal edge of triangles to the sashing, using a ¼" seam allowance. Press seam allowances toward triangles.

4. Fuse interfacing to plum speckled side gusset C on fabric wrong side.

5. Sew side gusset to sides and bottom edges of purse front, using a ¼" seam allowance, clipping the side gusset to seam line at the corners. Press seam allowance open.

6. Fuse interfacing to rust/plum striped back D. Sew side gusset to the sides and bottom edges of back in the same manner as in Step 5.

making lining

side view

1. Fuse the interfacing to one rust swirl front and back lining D piece.

2. Sew purple batik side gusset C lining piece to front and back lining pieces in the same manner as in Steps 5–6 above for sewing outer purse pieces together.

3. Slip lining into purse, wrong sides facing. Pin layers together at side gusset seam lines and purse top edges.

4. Fold purse along side gusset/front seam line. Topstitch a scant ⅛" from seam line along sides and bottom edges. At each corner, it will be necessary to break stitches and reposition the seam line.

5. Repeat Step 4 for side gusset/back seam line.

making handle

1. Cut two 24" lengths from ribbon.

2. Sew two lengths together along selvage edges. Do not stitch across short ends.

3. Wrap tape around cord at end and 16" from end. Cut cord through middle of tape.

4. Using safety pin attached to one cord end, slip cord through middle of ribbon. Hand-baste cord to entry end of ribbon. Exit cord at opposite end of ribbon and hand-baste cord in place at end. *Note: The ribbon will gather and twist around the cord, forming the handle.*

5. Pin handle ends to right side of purse centered at upper edges of side gusset. Hand-baste the ends in place.

making button loop

1. Working with remaining length of ribbon, fold ribbon in half, aligning selvages. Machine-sew the selvages together.

2. Fold ribbon in half, aligning ends and forming a loop. Pin the ends to right side of purse at center front.

finishing

1. Fuse interfacing to wrong side of binding strip E.

2. Sew short ends together, right sides facing, using a ¼" seam allowance. Press seam allowance open.

3. Pin and sew one long edge of binding around upper edge of the purse/lining, right sides facing, using a ¼" seam allowance and aligning the binding seam line at one side gusset/back seam line. Press seam allowance toward binding.

4. Press remaining raw edge of binding under ¼" to wrong side.

5. Fold binding strip over to enclose the seam allowance. Pin in place along folded-under edge.

6. Fold the ribbon loop upward onto binding. Pin in place.

7. Sew binding in place, catching ribbon loop in when sewing.

8. Sew handle onto binding at sides.

9. Hand-stitch button to center back of binding seam line.

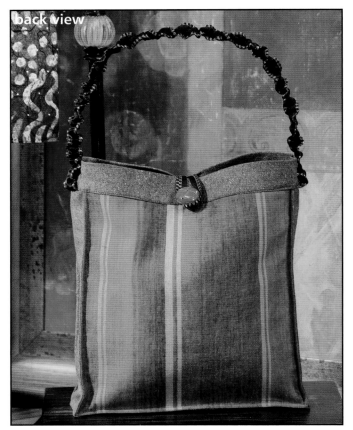

clarity patterns

Patterns on this page are actual size.

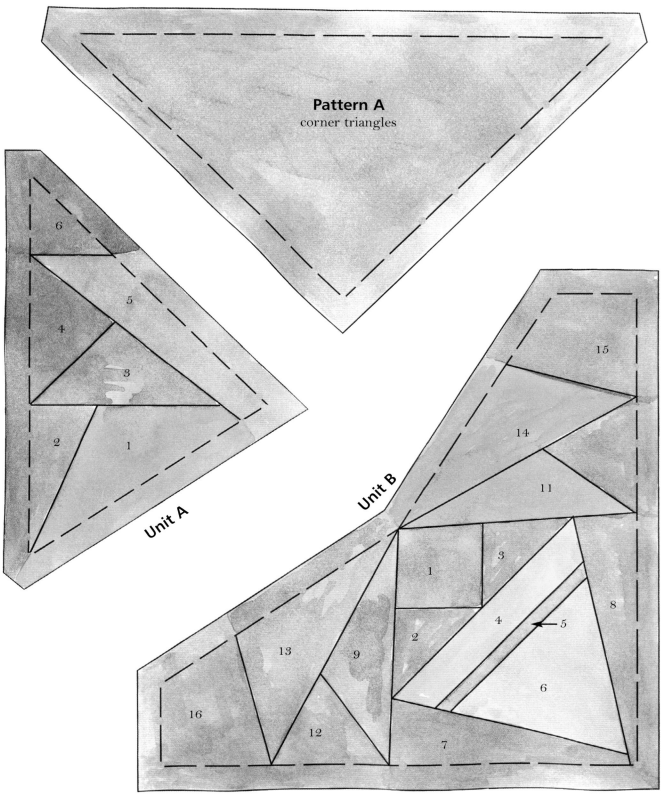

Pattern A
corner triangles

Unit A

Unit B

honesty

A fairness and straightforwardness of conduct. Refusal to lie, steal, or deceive in any way.

finished size
• 9" x 10"

cotton fabrics
Green (4 variations)
• 44"-wide light green geometric (⅜ yd) for front A; quilt backing/purse lining for front, back

• 44"-wide light green print (⅜ yd) for Pattern A

• 44"-wide light lime green floral (⅜ yd) for upper pocket B; lower pocket C

• 44"-wide turquoise floral (⅜ yd) for back A

Purple (2 variations)
• 44"-wide lavender floral (⅛ yd) for ruffle

• 44"-wide orchid geometric (⅛ yd) for ruffle

notions
• ¾" magnetic purse-bag closure
• 9" white nylon zipper
• 44"-wide cotton batting (⅜ yd)
• Lightweight fusible woven interfacing (5½" x 2½")
• Matching threads

tools
• General Tools on page 5
• Hand-sewing needle

cutting fabrics

Note: Enlarge Honesty Patterns on pages 55–56 200% unless otherwise indicated.

1. Using Pattern A, cut one piece from light green geometric fabric, cutting pieces ½" larger all around than pattern to allow for shrinkage due to quilting the fabric. Cut two pieces from light green print for front/back lining in the same manner.

2. Using Pattern A back, cut one piece from turquoise floral, cutting piece larger as in Step 1.

3. Cut one back binding strip 1¼" x 12" from turquoise floral. Cut one front binding/handle strip 1¼" x 32½" from turquoise floral. Cut two tab pieces 5½" x 2½" from turquoise floral.

4. Cut three ruffle strips 3½" x 44" from lavender floral and orchid geometric fabrics.

5. Using Pattern B, cut one upper pocket from light lime green floral.

6. Using Pattern C, cut one lower pocket from light lime green floral

7. Using Pattern A, cut two front/back pieces from batting, cutting pieces ½" larger all around than pattern.

8. Using water-soluble fabric-marking pen, mark all fabric pieces as indicated with pattern assembly markings. Refer to pattern pieces when assembling each purse.

quilting front and back

1. Place two light green print pieces for separately on work surface, wrong side up. Place batting pieces on top of each piece. Place light green geometric on one layered piece and turquoise floral on the remaining layered piece, right sides up. Pin each stacked layer together for one front and one back.

Continued on page 54.

53

Continued from page 52.

2. Using a free-motion machine-quilting technique, individually machine-quilt each layered stack.

3. Pin Pattern A to green geometric quilted front. Trim to pattern size. Repeat for turquoise floral quilted back.

making ruffled flower front

ruffled flower front

1. Piece the three lavender floral strips together along short the edges. Press seam allowances open.

2. Press under long edges of pieced-together strips ⅛" to fabric wrong side. Press strip in half, aligning pressed-under edges.

3. Machine-sew pressed-under edges together.

4. Repeat Steps 1–3 for two of orchid geometric strips. Repeat Steps 2–3 for remaining orchid geometric strip.

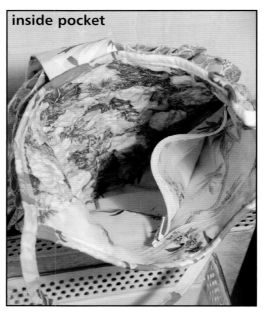
inside pocket

5. Using water-soluble fabric-marking pen, transfer concentric circle markings from Pattern A onto the purse front.

6. Using needle and doubled thread, gather-stitch lavender floral strip along sewn edge. Gather strip while stitching so that it shortens to about half of the original length.

7. Position gathered strip around third outer ring, then swirl strip onto second outer ring and into center ring. Adjust gathers as necessary. Coil end of strip more tightly at center ring to form a flower center.

8. When pleased with positioning of ruffle, stitch gathered edge to front, tucking raw ends under when stitching.

`9. Gather-stitch longer orchid geometric strip as in Step 6, gathering strip so that it shortens to about half of original length.

10. Position the gathered strip around outer ring, swirling end of strip onto third outer ring as far as it will go. Adjust gathers as necessary. Stitch gathered edge to front, tucking raw ends under when stitching.

11. Gather-stitch the remaining orchid geometric strip as in Step 6. Position gathered strip around center and second rings. When pleased with positioning of ruffle, stitch gathered edge to front, tucking raw ends under when stitching.

sewing front to back

1. Sew front to back along side and lower edges, right sides facing, using a ⅛" seam allowance. Make certain to move ruffle away from seam line when sewing. Press seam allowance toward back.

making inside zippered pocket

1. Working with upper pocket B and lower pocket C pieces, press straight fabric edge under ¾" to fabric wrong side. Pin pressed edge of upper pocket to left edge of the zipper tape, aligning fabric edge to edge of zipper coil.

2. Using a zipper foot, sew upper pocket pressed edge to zipper tape. Align and sew lower pocket pressed edge to opposite side of zipper tape in the same manner.

3. Turn straight edge under ¼" on underside. Double-stitch zipper to straight edge ⅛" from first row of stitching, catching in turned-under edge when sewing.

4. Press side and lower edges of assembled pocket under ½" to fabric wrong side.

5. Turn purse wrong side out.

6. Place wrong side of pocket over inside of back and pin in place, placing finished edge of pocket over seam line to enclose it and aligning upper edge of pocket with upper edge of back. Hand-stitch pocket in place along side and lower edges.

finishing

1. Bind upper edge of back with back binding strip, using a ¼" seam allowance.

2. Fuse interfacing to wrong side of one tab piece. Place tabs with right sides facing.

3. Fold one end diagonally on both sides and crease fabric. Using water-soluble pen, mark crease, indicating a pointed end on tab.

4. Sew the sides and pointed end of the tab, using a ¼" seam allowance. Trim excess fabric from pointed end.

5. Turn tab right side out. Push out corners and point. Press.

6. Apply smaller side of magnetic closure to inside of tab near pointed end. Apply opposite side of magnetic closure to back.

7. Pin tab to center front upper edge, right sides facing. Machine-baste in place.

8. Bind upper edge of front with front binding/ handle strip, using a ¼" seam allowance. Begin with a turned-under end at center front, sewing binding to right upper edge. Measure 19" on strip from right upper edge for handle portion of strip. Place a pin to mark measurement.

9. Continue binding upper edge of front with remainder of strip, overlapping end onto beginning end of strip at upper edge of front.

10. Press under both edges of handle portion of strip ¼" to fabric wrong side. Press handle portion in half, aligning pressed-under edges.

11. Hand-stitch binding in place, stitching along pressed-under edges of handle in the process.

back view

honesty pattern

Enlarge pattern on this page 200%.

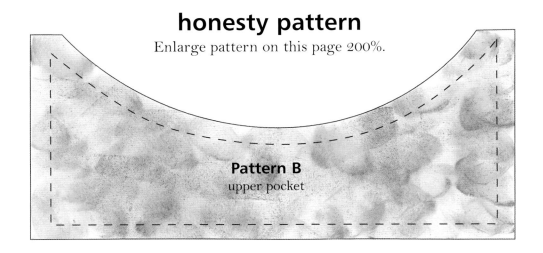

Pattern B
upper pocket

honesty patterns

Enlarge patterns on this page 200%.

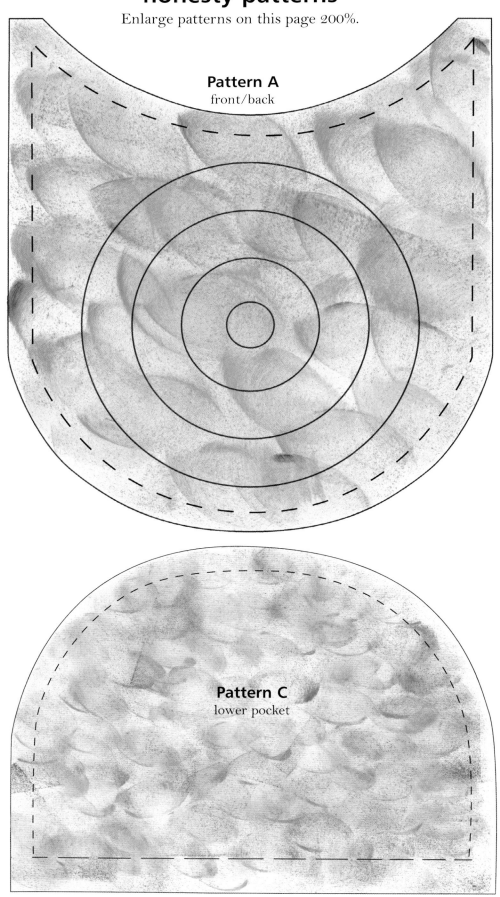

Pattern A
front/back

Pattern C
lower pocket

bliss

An emotion of complete happiness, paradise, heaven.

Bliss photo shown on page 60.

finished size
• 7" x 8" x 4¼"

cotton fabrics

Gray (2 variations)
• 44"-wide gray broadcloth (¼ yd) for A; B; vertical stripes; horizontal stripe; zipper strip; handle

Pink (2 variations)
• 44"-wide mauve-pink broadcloth (½ yd) for A; vertical stripes; lower body backing
• 44"-wide pink broadcloth (¼ yd) for A; C; lid strip; appliquéd heart

White (1 variation)
• White fleece (9" x 5") for appliquéd wings; appliquéd heart

embellishments
• ⅛"-wide pink picot trim (½ yd)

notions
• 20" pink zipper
• 44"-wide cotton batting (¼ yd)
• Bright rose machine-embroidery thread
• Matching threads

tools
• General Tools on page 5
• Crescent board (8" x 20")
• Large safety pin
• Needles: hand-sewing; machine-embroidery
• Quilter's freezer paper
• Tacky glue

cutting fabrics and crescent board

Note: Enlarge Bliss Patterns on pages 61–62 200% unless otherwise indicated.

1. Using Pattern A, cut one, ½" larger all around than pattern from mauve-pink broadcloth. Cut nine 1½" x 6" strips from mauve-pink broadcloth. Cut one lower body backing piece 8" x 19" from mauve-pink broadcloth.

2. Using Pattern A, cut two ½" larger all around than pattern from pink broadcloth. Cut one pleated pocket C from pink broadcloth. Cut one lid strip 4½" x 19" from pink broadcloth.

3. Using Pattern A, cut one 1" larger all around than pattern from gray broadcloth. Cut nine 1½" x 6" strips from gray broadcloth. Using Pattern B, cut one lining for pocket foundation from gray broadcloth. Cut one horizontal strip 3" x 19" from gray broadcloth. Cut two zipper strips 1¼" x 3" from gray broadcloth. Cut one handle 1¼" x 18" from gray broadcloth.

4. Using Pattern A, cut one from cotton batting. Cut one lower body quilting piece 8" x 19" from cotton batting. Cut one lid strip 2¼" x 19" from cotton batting.

5. Using Pattern A, cut four from crescent board.

6. Using water-soluble fabric-marking pen, mark all fabric pieces as indicated with the patterns assembly markings. Refer to pattern pieces when assembling each purse.

piecing purse lower body

1. Alternating fabrics, sew nine mauve-pink and gray strips together, aligning 6" edges and using a ¼" seam allowance, creating striped fabric. Press seam allowances toward gray strips. Do not join last strip to first strip.

2. Sew gray horizontal strip to one long edge of striped fabric, forming lower body of purse. Press seam allowance toward gray horizontal strip.

machine-quilting purse lower body and appliquéing flying heart

1. Place mauve-pink lower body backing piece on work surface, wrong side up. Place lower body batting piece over it. Position pieced lower body over batting, right side up.

2. Using a free-motion machine-quilting technique, machine-quilt the vertical strips.

3. Using Wing Pattern, cut two from white fleece. Using Large Heart Pattern, cut one from the white fleece.

4. Using Small Heart Pattern, cut one from freezer paper. Press shiny side of freezer paper face downward onto wrong side of a piece of pink broadcloth. Trim broadcloth with a ¼" seam allowance around the paper pattern.

5. Spray some starch into lid or small container. Saturate cotton swab with spray starch. Dab outer edge of fabric with swab. Clip outer edge of fabric up to freezer paper. Using iron on steam, press outer edges of fabric up over edge of freezer paper, being careful to maintain the heart shape. Remove freezer paper and press again.

6. Position and pin fleece wings and heart along gray horizontal strip seam line, centering wings and heart over the fifth mauve-pink strip from right side of lower body.

7. Pin broadcloth heart centered over fleece heart. Stitch broadcloth heart in place.

8. Continue machine-quilting lower body, beginning with flying heart, then continuing with the rest of gray horizontal strip.

machine-embroidering purse lower body

1. Using water-soluble fabric-marking pen, write in cursive "from the heart" 1" upward from bottom center of quilted lower body.

2. Using bright rose machine-embroidery thread, free-motion embroider lettering.

3. Free-motion quilt around wings and heart with small picot-edged-appearing stitches.

4. Press under upper edge of quilted lower body ¾" to wrong side.

preparing lid strip and applying zipper to purse

1. Press the pink broadcloth lid strip in half lengthwise. Open-out.

2. With fabric wrong side up, place one long edge of batting lid strip on pressed line. Refold on pressed line.

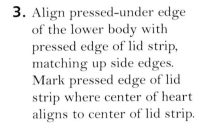

3. Align pressed-under edge of the lower body with pressed edge of lid strip, matching up side edges. Mark pressed edge of lid strip where center of heart aligns to center of lid strip.

4. Using water-soluble fabric-marking pen, write in capital letters "BEAUTY", ¼" upward from folded edge of strip and centered on lid strip where indicated by mark from Step 3.

5. Using bright rose machine-embroidery thread, free-motion embroider lettering. Machine-quilt the rest of lid strip.

6. Pin pressed edge of lower body to left edge of zipper tape, aligning fabric edge to edge of zipper coil. Using a zipper foot, machine-sew pressed edge of lower body to zipper tape. Align and sew lid strip to opposite side of zipper tape in the same manner.

7. Fold zippered body in half, aligning side edges. Sew side edges together, using a ¼" seam allowance. Press seam allowance open. Trim excess zipper ½" past seam allowance.

8. Using one zipper strip, press long edges under ¼" to fabric wrong side. Press short edges under ½" to wrong side.

9. Working from outside of body, position zipper strip over zipper coil, aligning one short edge up with zipper pull and extending the rest of strip over seam line and onto zipper coil that is the end of zipper. Sew zipper strip in place. Turn inside out.

10. Using remaining zipper strip, press long edges under ¼" to wrong side. Working from inside of body, position strip over lid strip seam line and over seamed-together zipper pull/coil, aligning it with outer strip from Step 9 on page 58. Hand-stitch pressed-under edges in place.

making inside pleated pocket

1. Press pleated pocket piece in half where indicated on pattern.

2. Align stitch lines on lining (pocket foundation) with stitch lines on pleated pocket piece. Pin in place. Align sides of lining piece with sides of pleated pocket piece.

3. Sew pleated pocket piece to lining piece along the stitch lines. Machine-baste the side edges together.

4. Form box pleats with excess fabric from pleated pocket piece at each stitch line, folding pleats in direction of arrows indicated on pleated pocket pattern.

5. Machine-baste lower edges together.

6. Fold assembled pocket in half, right sides facing, aligning side edges. Sew side edges together, using a ¼" seam allowance. Press seam allowance open. Turn upper edge of pocket foundation under ½" to wrong side.

7. Slip pocket piece over purse, wrong sides facing, aligning bottom edge of pocket piece with bottom edge of lower body and positioning turned under edge ¼" downward from zipper coil.

8. Hand-stitch turned-under edge in place. Turn purse body right side out.

making handle

handle

1. Press long edges of handle under ¼" to wrong side. Press handle in half, aligning pressed-under edges.

2. Sew pressed-under edges together.

3. Stitch pink picot trim to one edge of handle.

finishing

1. Cover one crescent board for bottom with mauve-pink piece A, gluing excess fabric around crescent with the glue. Cover second crescent board for bottom with one of pink piece A in the same manner. Cover one crescent board piece for top with remaining pink piece A.

2. Turn bottom edge of lower body under ½" to inside of purse. Hand-baste turned-under edge in place.

3. Stitch outer edge of the mauve-pink covered piece to turned-under edge of lower body, working from outside of purse, forming bottom of purse.

4. Slip and adhere one of pink covered crescent board piece into bottom inside.

5. Layer gray piece A with cotton batting. Using a free-motion machine-quilting technique, machine-quilt layers together.

6. Cover remaining top crescent board piece with quilted piece A, gluing excess fabric around the crescent board.

7. Turn top edge of lid strip under ½" to inside of purse. Hand-baste turned-under edge in place.

8. Position ends of handle at sides of lid strip. Stitch ends to inside edge of lid strip at sides.

9. Stitch outer edge of quilted gray piece to turned-under edge of lid strip, working from outside of purse.

10. Slip and adhere remaining pink covered piece into inside lid of purse.

bliss patterns

Enlarge patterns on this page 200%.

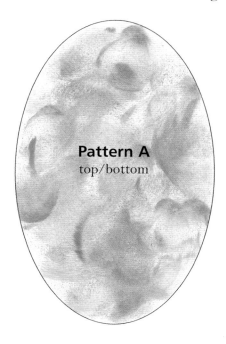

Pattern A
top/bottom

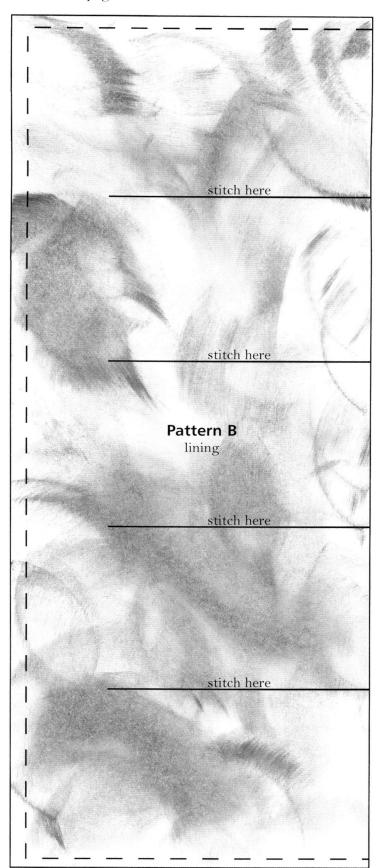

stitch here

stitch here

Pattern B
lining

stitch here

stitch here

bliss patterns

Enlarge patterns on this page as indicated.

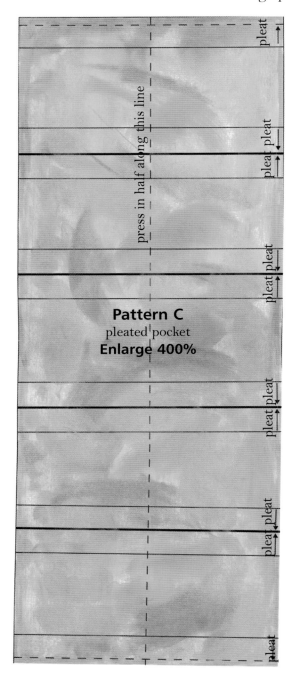

Pattern C
pleated pocket
Enlarge 400%

pleat

press in half along this line

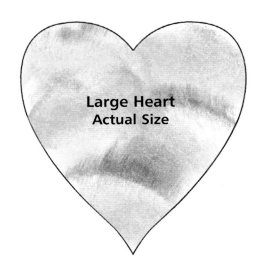

**Large Heart
Actual Size**

**Small Heart
Actual Size**

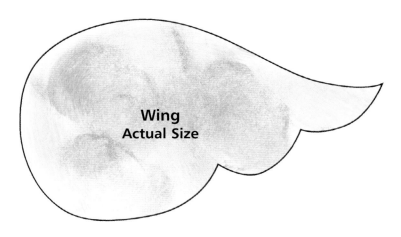

**Wing
Actual Size**

medium purses

A bag or tote in the middle range. Being intermediate in amount or position.

energy
A vigorous exertion of power.

finished size
• 14" (top) x 10" (bottom) x 9½"

embellishments
• ½"-wide fuchsia rickrack (⅞ yd)
• ½"wide light blue rickrack (1½ yd)
• ½"-wide orange rickrack (¾ yd)
• ¾"-wide rectangle rings (4)
• 1½"-wide light blue velvet ribbon (1⅛ yd)

cotton fabrics
• 44"-wide marigold/yellow polka-dot (¼ yd) for Pattern D; Pattern E
• 44"-wide orchid floral (⅞ yd) for zippered pocket underlay Pattern A; Pattern H; Pattern I; Pattern J; Pattern K; rectangle ring pieces
• 44"-wide orange/red polka-dot (⅛ yd) for Pattern C
• 44"-wide red/orange/pink multi (¼ yd) for Pattern B; Pattern F; Pattern G
• 44"-wide orange variegated polka-dot (⅛ yd) for Pattern A

notions
• 9" peach zippers (2)
• 12" red zipper
• 22"-wide medium-weight fusible woven interfacing (⅜ yd)
• 44"-wide cotton batting (½ yd)
• Matching threads

tools
• General Tools on page 5
• Hand-sewing needle
• Large safety pin
• Masking tape

cutting fabrics

Note: Enlarge Energy Patterns on pages 69–73 200% unless otherwise indicated.

1. Using Pattern A, cut two for front and back from variegated orange with red polka-dots cotton fabric. Cut two from cotton batting. Cut two for front and back zippered pocket underlay from orchid floral cotton fabric.

2. Using Pattern B, cut two outer pocket lower strips for front and back, using red/orange/pink multi cotton fabric.

3. Using Pattern C, cut two outer pocket middle strips for front and back, using orange/red polka-dot cotton fabric.

4. Using Pattern D, cut two outer pocket top strips for front and back, using marigold/yellow polka-dot cotton fabric.

5. Using Pattern E, cut two outer pocket lining pieces for front and back, using marigold/yellow polka-dot cotton fabric. Cut two from cotton batting.

6. Using Pattern F, cut two for base and base lining, using red/orange/pink multi cotton fabric. Cut one from cotton batting.

7. Using Pattern G, cut two for the inner flat pockets using red/orange/pink multi cotton fabric. Cut two 7" x 6½" from fusible interfacing.

8. Using Pattern H, cut two for upper zippered pocket front and back (also becomes lining), using the orchid floral cotton fabric.

9. Using Pattern I, cut two for lower zippered pocket front and back (also becomes lining), using the orchid floral cotton fabric.

10. Using Pattern J , cut two closure strips from orchid floral cotton fabric. Cut two 9" x 2½" from fusible interfacing.

11. Using Pattern K, cut two tabs from orchid floral cotton fabric. Cut one from fusible interfacing.

Continued on page 66.

Continued from page 64.

12. Cut one end strip for zippered pockets 1¼" x 12" from orchid floral cotton fabric. Cut one 2½" x 10" piece for rectangle ring from the orchid floral cotton fabric.

13. Using water-soluble fabric-marking pen, mark all fabric pieces as indicated with the patterns assembly markings. Refer to pattern pieces when assembling each purse. *Note: Seam allowances are ½" unless noted.*

making outer pockets

1. Machine-sew orange rickrack trim to wider edge of outer pocket middle C strips along seam line. Sew fuchsia rickrack trim to wider edge of outer pocket top D strips along seam line. Sew light blue rickrack trim to narrower edge of B outer pocket lower strips along seam line.

2. Sew wider edge of one outer pocket lower strip B to narrower edge of one outer pocket middle C strip, right sides facing. Press seam allowance toward lower strip. Repeat with other outer pocket lower and middle strip pieces.

3. Sew narrower edge of one outer pocket strip D to wider edge of one outer pocket middle C strip C, right sides facing. Press seam allowance toward middle strip, forming right side of one outer pocket. Repeat with remaining top strip. (See Illus. A)

Illus. A

4. Place one outer pocket batting piece E against wrong side of one assembled outer pocket. Place one outer pocket lining E piece E with one assembled outer pocket, right sides facing.

5. Sew pieces together along upper (widest) edge. Trim batting just past seam line. Press seam allowance toward outer pocket. Turn so that wrong sides are facing. Press top edge flat.

6. Repeat for the second outer pocket pieces. (See Illus. B)

7. Using a free-motion machine-quilting technique, machine-quilt the two outer pockets.

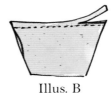

Illus. B

assembling purse at side seams

1. Place batting A pieces on wrong side of front and back A pieces. Using a free-motion machine-quilting technique, machine-quilt the front and back pieces.

2. Pin lining side of quilted outer pockets onto right side of quilted front and back, aligning bottom and side edges.

3. Sew finished upper edge of outer pockets to front and back, sewing from the side edges to dots indicated on Pattern A front/back.

4. Sew front layered with outer pocket to back layered with outer pocket along the side edges, right sides facing, matching the outer pocket strip seam lines. Press seam allowances open.

5. Sew light blue rickrack over the side seams.

6. Working with rectangle ring strip, press both long edges under ½" to fabric wrong side. Press strip in half, aligning pressed-under edges. Sew along both long edges.

7. Cut strip into four 2½" lengths.

inner pockets

8. Slip one cut length through one rectangle ring. Fold length in half, aligning cut ends and enclosing ring. Pin ends together. Repeat with other lengths and rectangle rings.

9. Pin ends to upper edge of front and back, right sides facing, between dots indicated on Pattern A front/back for ring strip placement.

10. Hand-baste the ends in place along seam line.

making inner flat pockets

1. Refer to Pattern G on page 72. Fuse the inner pocket interfacing pieces to the wrong side of each inner flat pocket fabric piece where indicated on the pattern.

2. Fold pocket in half along fold line, right sides facing. Sew side edges, using a ¼" seam allowance. Turn right side out. Press.

3. Sew flat pockets to lower zippered pocket fabric pieces I where indicated on pattern, making certain to sew along upper edge, then diagonally as shown on pattern. (See Illus. C) *Note: This additional sewing on the pocket will keep the pocket from falling open inside the purse.*

Illus. C

making zippered pockets

1. Working with upper H and lower zippered pocket I pieces, press fabric edge (for zipper placement) under ¼" to fabric wrong side. Working with a 9" zipper between dots for zipper placement, pin pressed edge of upper pocket to left edge of zipper tape, aligning pressed fabric edge to edge of zipper coil, beginning and ending zipper at dots. Using a zipper foot, machine-sew upper pocket pressed edges to zipper tape. Align and sew lower pocket pressed edge to the opposite side of the zipper tape in the same manner. Sew again ⅛" from first row of stitching along both edges of zipper.

2. Press long edges of the 1¼" x 12" zipper end strip under ¼" to the wrong side. Cut the strip into four 3" lengths. Sew one short end of strip to end of zipper and upper/lower pocket pieces, with right sides facing, using a ¼" seam allowance with the strip. Fold strip over to extend past side edges of pocket pieces. Topstitch along the top, inner edge, and bottom on the strip through all layers. Repeat for remaining end of zipper, making a clean and sturdy finish for zippered pocket.

3. Repeat Steps 1–2 for second pocket. *Note: The zippered pockets become the purse lining.*

making closure strips

1. Fuse closure strip interfacing pieces centered to wrong side of closure strip fabric J pieces.

2. Press under short ends indicated on pattern.

3. Press one strip in half, right sides facing, aligning long edges. Sew across short end indicated on pattern. Clip bulk from corner. Turn right side out. Press. Repeat with the remaining strip.

4. Pin folded edge of one strip (starting with pressed-under end) to left edge of zipper tape, aligning fabric edge to edge of zipper coil and placing top stop at pressed-under end. *Note: The zipper will extend beyond the remaining end of the strip.*

5. Fold excess from top stop end of zipper tape to within pressed-under edge of strip (See Illus. D)

Illus. D

6. Using a zipper foot, sew across pressed-under end of strip, along folded edge of strip/zipper tape, and across sewn end of strip. Sew again along folded edge a scant ¼" from first row of stitching, catching outer edge of zipper tape when sewing. Repeat with remaining side of zipper coil and closure strip. (See Illus. E)

Illus. E

7. Fuse interfacing to wrong side of one tab fabric K piece. Place two tab fabric pieces with right sides facing. Sew side and curved edges, using a ¼" seam allowance. Clip seam allowance at curved edge to seam line, but not through stitches. Edge-press seam allowance open. Turn right side out.

8. Turn under open edges of tab ¼" to inside. Press.

9. Slip end of zipper through open side of tab. Sew across open end and through zipper.

10. Fold tab in half along straight end. Stitch ends together for a decorative tab finish.

applying closure strips to lining

1. Refer to Pattern H for upper zippered pocket. *Note: There is a stitch line for closure strips positioned between two dots and is indicated on pattern by "Sew closure strips along here." Mark this line on upper zippered pocket portion of lining fabric pieces on right side of fabric, using disappearing ink pen.*

2. Both sides of closure strips with applied zipper have one raw edge. With right sides facing, position seam line from one raw edge onto marked line. (See Illus. F) Sew closure strip to marked line. Sew

Illus. F

again ¼" from first row of stitching. Trim seam allowance from closure strip close to second row of stitching. Machine-overcast seam allowance and through all layers.

3. Position seam line from raw edge of remaining closure strip with applied zipper onto marked line. Sew as with Step 2. (See Illus. G)

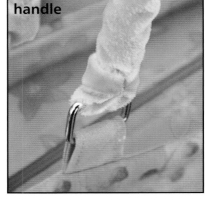
Illus. G

4. With right sides facing, sew lining side seams. Press seam allowances open.

finishing purse upper edge

1. Place lining over the purse with right sides facing, aligning the upper edges and matching the side seams.

2. Sew around upper edges. Press seam allowance toward lining. Topstitch ¼" from seam line onto the lining and through seam allowance layers.

3. Slip lining to inside of purse. Press upper edges.

4. Smooth lining within purse. *Note: The lower edges of the lining will extend past the lower edges of the purse.* Trim excess fabric from lower edges of lining, then baste-stitch lining to purse along lower edges. Clip the seam allowance to seam line, making certain to first mark the center front, the center back, and side seam markings.

sewing base to purse lower edges

1. Sandwich base batting F piece between base fabric F pieces with wrong sides facing.

2. Turn purse with lining side out.

3. Pin outer fabric lower edge of purse to outer edge of layered base pieces, with right sides facing, matching the center front, center back, and side seam markings.

4. Sew base to lower edge of purse, working from purse side. Sew again ⅛" from first row of stitching. Trim seam allowance just past second row of stitching. Overcast seam allowance. (See Illus. H) Turn purse right side out.

Illus. H

finishing

1. Cut velvet ribbon into two 20" lengths. Mark 2" from each end on both lengths.

2. Fold one ribbon length in half, aligning long edges, wrong sides facing. Using a very narrow zigzag stitch, machine-sew selvage edges together, sewing only between 2" end marks. Repeat with remaining ribbon length.

3. Measure a 16" length on the cord. Wrap masking tape around cord end and around 16" mark. Trim cord by cutting through middle of the tape. Repeat for another 16" length.

4. Pin and close safety pin through one cord end. Using safety pin, slip cord through one end of ribbon tube. When opposite cord end aligns with 2" mark on ribbon, sew end of cord securely to ribbon at mark. Repeat with remaining cord end at opposite 2" mark on ribbon, forming ribbon handle. Repeat with second lengths of ribbon and cord.

5. Slip one ribbon end through one rectangle ring. Fold ribbon end under ¼" to ribbon wrong side (See Illus. I), then wrap folded-under end around ribbon where cord has been stitched to it. Hand-stitch folded-under ends together and to ribbon handle. Make certain to remove safety pin.

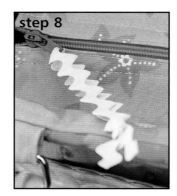
Illus. I

6. Repeat Step 6 for remaining end of ribbon handle, working from same side of purse.

7. Repeat Steps 5–6 with remaining ribbon handle.

8. Cut 8" length from light blue rickrack. Slip one end through zipper pull on closure strips. Fold rickrack in half and tie ends together. Coat ends with fray preventative. Trim ends at a slant when fray preventative has dried.

energy pattern

Enlarge pattern on this page 200%.

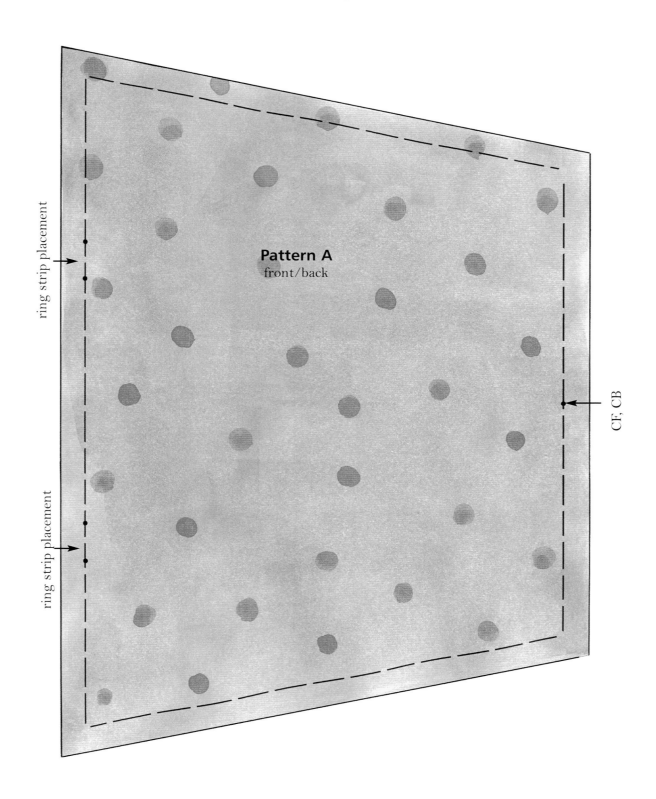

Pattern A
front/back

ring strip placement

ring strip placement

CF, CB

energy patterns

Enlarge pattern on this page 200%.

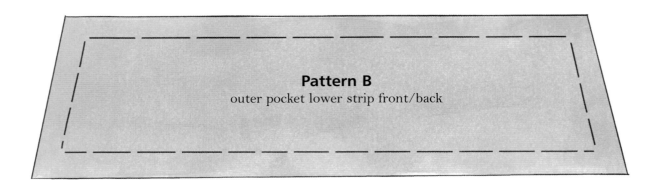

Pattern B
outer pocket lower strip front/back

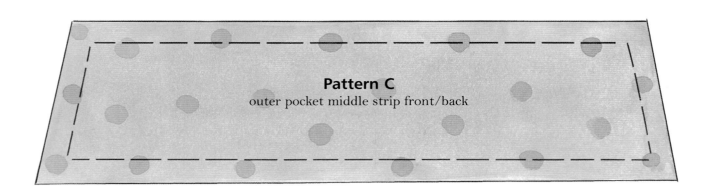

Pattern C
outer pocket middle strip front/back

stitch pocket to
front/back to dots

stitch pocket to
front/back to dots

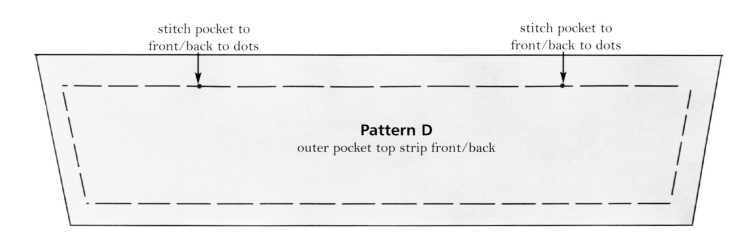

Pattern D
outer pocket top strip front/back

energy patterns

Enlarge pattern on this page 200%.

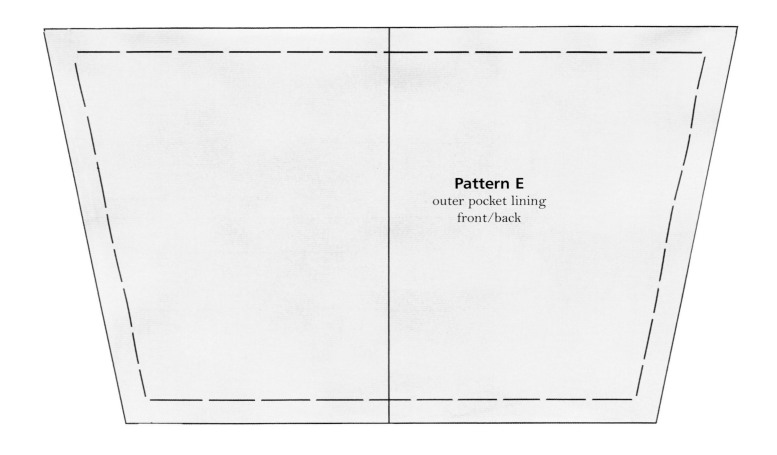

Pattern E
outer pocket lining
front/back

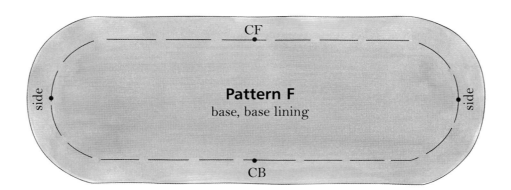

CF

side

Pattern F
base, base lining

side

CB

energy patterns

Enlarge patterns on this page 200%.

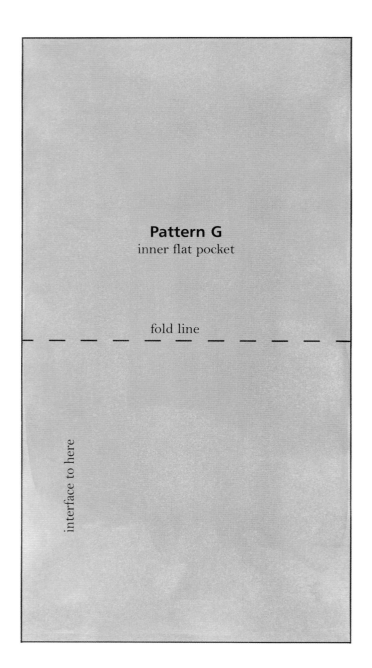

Pattern G
inner flat pocket

fold line

interface to here

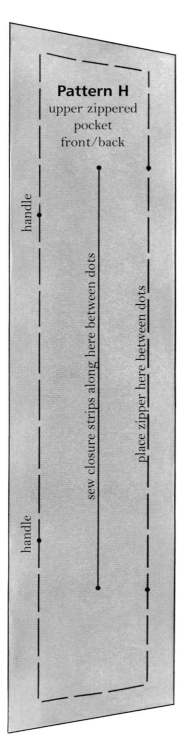

Pattern H
upper zippered
pocket
front/back

handle

handle

sew closure strips along here between dots

place zipper here between dots

energy patterns

Enlarge patterns on this page 200%.

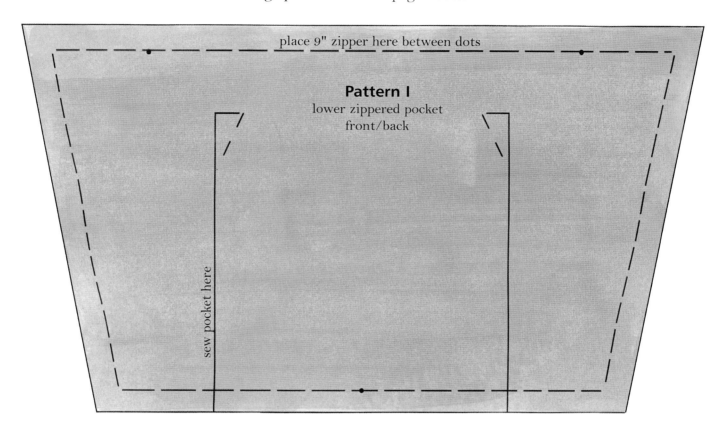

place 9" zipper here between dots

Pattern I
lower zippered pocket
front/back

sew pocket here

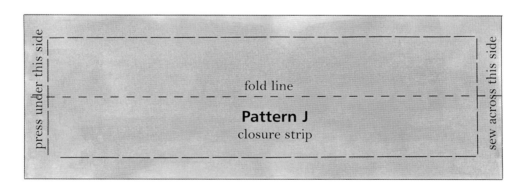

press under this side

fold line

Pattern J
closure strip

sew across this side

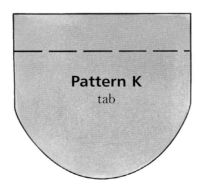

Pattern K
tab

sweet simplicity

The freedom from pretense or guile. A sweet pleasing of the mind.

finished size

• 12" x 13"

embellishments

• ⅜₆" black ball button
• ⅜"-wide bright rose picot-edged ribbon (¼ yd)
• ⅜" dia. white cord (½ yd)
• 1½"-wide pink ombré ribbon (⅔ yd)
• 8/0 pink seed beads (8)
• 14/0 burgundy seed beads (6)
• 2mm pearls (8)
• 4mm lime green silk ribbon (¼ yd)
• 6mm green flower-shaped beads (6)
• 6mm pink tulip-shaped beads (6)
• 12mm-long pink rice-shaped beads (18)
• Embroidery flosses: black; bright rose
• Hot-pink pom-pom trim (⅝ yd)

fabrics

Black/white (1 variation)
• 44"-wide black/white striped cotton (⅛ yd) for appliqués #1, #2

Bright pink (4 variations)
• 44"-wide bright pink cotton batik (⅛ yd) for appliqués #7, #11
• 44"-wide coral cotton batik (⅛ yd) for appliqué #12; front appliqué portion upper strip; front upper striped portion D; B flap #1
• 44"-wide fuchsia small print cotton (⅛ yd) for appliqués #3, #8
• 44"-wide pink heart cotton batik (¾ yd) for Pattern A; appliqués #4, #13; B flap

Green (5 variations)
• 44"-wide apple green cotton-blend poplin (½ yd) for front upper striped portions B and C, back side striped portion A; inside flat pocket; B flaps #2, and #4
• 44"-wide green cotton batik (⅛ yd) for appliqués #9, #10; leaves
• 44"-wide light green cotton batik (⅛ yd) for appliqué #7; leaves
• 44"-wide light olive linen (½ yd) for appliqué #6; front upper striped portion A; back middle striped portion B; B flap #3
• 44"-wide pale olive tone-on-tone paisley cotton (⅛ yd) for appliqué #5; leaves

White (3 variations)
• 40"-wide white organza (⅛ yd) for appliqués #1, #2
• 44"-wide white linen (⅜ yd) for front appliqué portion
• 44"−72"-wide ivory tulle (⅜ yd) for front appliqué portion

notions

• ¾" magnetic purse-bag closure
• 12" black zipper
• 22"-wide medium-weight fusible woven interfacing (½ yd)
• 44"-wide cotton batting (½ yd)
• Threads: black; matching; white

tools

• General Tools on page 5
• Fine-tipped permanent ink fabric-marking pen
• Large safety pin
• Needles: beading or milliners; embroidery sizes 3, 5; hand-sewing
• Tacky glue

cutting front and lining fabrics

Note: Enlarge Sweet Simplicity Patterns on pages 80–82 as indicated.

1. Using Pattern A for overall purse body shape, cut three from pink heart cotton batik fabric for front pocket lining and purse lining. Cut one from cotton batting and fusible interfacing.

2. For appliquéd portion of front, cut one 13½" x 11½" piece from the white linen. *Note: This piece is trimmed to 13" x 11" once appliquéd, quilted and embroidered.* Cut one each 13½" x 11½" from ivory tulle and cotton batting.

3. For upper stripe on appliquéd portion of front, cut one 13" x 11⅞" from coral cotton batik.

4. For upper striped portion of front wider stripes A, cut three 3½" x 3⅝" pieces from the light olive linen.

5. For upper striped portion of front narrower stripes B and C, cut two B 1¼" x 3⅝" pieces and two C 3⅝" x 1½" pieces from apple poplin.

6. For lower stripe on upper striped portion of front D, cut one 13" x 4¼" piece from coral batik.

7. Using water-soluble fabric-marking pen, mark all fabric pieces as indicated with the patterns assembly markings. Refer to pattern pieces when assembling each purse.

cutting purse back, flap, and inside flat pocket fabrics

1. For back side stripes A, cut two 4¾" x 14½" pieces from apple poplin.

2. For back middle stripe B, cut one 4½" x 14½" piece from light olive linen.

3. Using Pattern B for flap, cut one each from pink heart cotton batik, cotton batting, and fusible interfacing.

4. For striped flap top stripe (#1), cut one 13" x 1½" x piece from coral batik.

5. For striped flap narrow strips (#2, #4), cut one (#2) 13" x 1¼" piece and one (#4) 13" x 1½" piece from apple poplin.

6. For striped flap wide strip (#3), cut one 13" x 3½" piece from light olive linen.

7. For inside flat pocket, cut one 10" x 18" piece from apple poplin.

appliquéd front cutting technique

1. Cut out each of the appliqué pattern pieces along the outlines.

2. Place appliqué pattern pieces with their corresponding fabrics. Spray-starch each piece of fabric for amount needed to cut out appliqué pieces.

3. Trace appliqué pieces upside down onto each piece of fabric.

4. Cut out the appliqué pieces from the fabrics as indicated below:

a. Using Appliqué Patterns #1 and #2, cut one of each from black/white striped fabric.

b. Repeat Step 1 with white organza fabric.

c. Using Appliqué Patterns #3 and #8, cut one of each from the fuchsia small print fabric.

d. Using Appliqué Pattern #4, cut one from pink heart cotton batik. Cut ⅛" x 4½" piece along bias of fabric for appliqué #13.

e. Using Appliqué Pattern #5, cut one piece from pale olive paisley cotton.

f. Using Leaf Pattern, cut 12 leaves from pale olive tone-on-tone paisley cotton.

g. Using Appliqué Pattern #6, cut one piece from light olive linen.

h. Using Appliqué Patterns #7 and #11, cut one of each from bright pink batik.

i. Using Appliqué Pattern #7, cut one piece from light green batik.

j. Using the Leaf Pattern, cut leaves 12 from light green batik.

k. Using Appliqué Patterns #9 and #10, cut one of each from the green batik.

l. Using Leaf Pattern, cut 12 leaves from the green batik.

m. Using Appliqué Pattern #12, cut one piece from coral batik.

appliquéing and quilting front

1. Using water-soluble fabric-marking pen, transfer some of design placement lines onto white linen piece for appliqué portion of front.

2. Using very small finger-dabs of glue, adhere appliqué pieces to linen in numerical order.

(See Illus. A) *Note: The organza pieces are placed over the black/white striped pieces to tone down the boldness of the stripe.* For door awning, off-set bright pink and light green batik pieces so that there is a narrow border of the bright pink showing. Do not place the bed of leaves at this time.

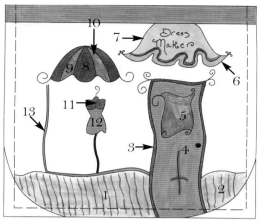

Illus. A

3. On the door and using permanent ink fabric marker, write store hours on window (appliqué #5): Hours: Open: Late. Close: Early. Using iron, heat-set ink.

4. Place piece of batting on underside of linen. Place piece of tulle over front of linen/appliqué pieces.

5. Machine-quilt around appliqué pieces and over Appliqué Pieces #1 and #2 with white thread, using a free-motion machine-quilting method.

6. Using free-motion quilting method, machine-quilt around outer edges of appliqué pieces with black thread, creating a thin "drawn" outline effect.

embroidering details on appliquéd front

1. Using water-soluble fabric-marking pen, draw embroidered detailing on the appliquéd front.

2. Using embroidery needle and couching stitch, embroider curlique detailing for umbrella awning, dress-form stand, and one above door swirls with six strands of black floss.

3. Using Backstitch on page 9, create dress form curlique detailing, door awning curliques, other above-the-door swirls and swirls around window with two strands of black floss.

4. Straight-stitch a bit of store hours with two strands of black floss.

5. Using backstitch, embroider "Dress Maker" on door awning with three strands of bright rose floss.

finishing appliquéd front details

1. Position leaves along upper edge of Appliqué Pieces #1 and #2. Machine-quilt leaves in place, using a free-motion machine-quilting method,

catching raw edges of leaves when sewing.

2. Trim appliquéd front piece to 13" x 11".

3. Sew pink rice-shaped beads to the leaf bed in a letter "V" formation.

4. Sew green flower-shaped beads to leaf bed, anchoring each with a burgundy seed bead. Sew pearls to dress form.

5. Sew tulip-shaped beads to lower edge o door awning as follows:

a. Bring needle to surface near left side lower edge of awning. Slip tulip bead onto needle. Move bead to meet fabric entry point.

b. Slip 8/0 seed bead onto needle. Stitch around seed bead, then back through tulip bead and into fabric at entry point.

c. Take a tiny stitch at entry point to anchor thread, then invisibly stitch about 1" away from entry point to the next spot for beading on the lower edge of the awning. Continue to bead lower edge of awning. *Note: Vary the bead lengths by using a seed bead before slipping the tulip bead on the needle, or by using two seed beads after the tulip bead has been slipped on the needle.*

6. Sew 13" x 11⅜" piece of coral batik to upper edge of appliquéd front, aligning 13" edges, right sides facing, using a ¼" seam allowance. Press seam allowance toward coral fabric.

7. Measure ⅜" on coral batik from seam line. Fold and press fabric on mark, folding fabric to the back side of appliquéd front, creating it's backing. Pin in place. (See Illus. B)

Illus. B

making front upper striped portion

1. Sew poplin B pieces to left edge of two linen A pieces, right sides facing, using a ¼" seam allowance. Press seam allowances open.

2. Sew one poplin C piece to right edge of third linen piece, right sides facing, using a ¼" seam allowance. Sew other poplin C piece to left edge of first linen piece, right sides facing, using a ¼" seam allowance. Press seam allowances open.

3. Sew pieces together to create stripes, having wider poplin pieces at right and left sides. Press seam allowances open.

4. Sew 4¼" x 13" D coral batik to lower edge of striped piece, aligning the 3" edges, right sides facing, using a ¼" seam allowance. Press seam allowance toward coral fabric. (See Illus. C)

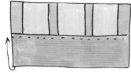

Illus. C

5. Measure ⅜" on coral batik from the seam line. Fold and press fabric on the mark, folding fabric to back side of striped piece. Pin in place.

making zippered front pocket

1. Working with appliquéd front piece, pin folded edge of coral batik upper strip to left edge of zipper tape, aligning folded fabric edge to edge of zipper coil. Using a zipper foot, machine-sew folded edge to zipper tape. Sew again a scant ¼" from first row of stitching, catching in edge of zipper tape when sewing.

2. Working with striped piece, pin and sew folded edge of coral batik lower strip to opposite side of zipper tape in the same manner. Sew again a scant ¼" from first row of stitching in the same manner as Step 1.

3. Place pink heart batik A piece against wrong side of assembled front piece. Pin and machine-baste layers together along outer edges, using a ½" seam allowance.

making back

1. Sew poplin pieces for back A to right and left edges of linen piece for back B, aligning 14½" edges, right sides facing, using a ¼" seam allowance. Press seam allowances open.

2. Place batting on wrong side of the back. Pin and machine-baste layers together, using a ½" seam allowance.

making flap

1. Sew coral flap stripe #1 to poplin flap stripe #2 along the 13" edges, right sides facing, using a ¼" seam allowance.

2. Sew linen flap stripe #3 to poplin flap stripe #4 along 13" edges, right sides facing, using a ¼" seam allowance.

3. Sew poplin edge from Step 1 to linen edge from Step 2, right sides facing, using a ¼" seam allowance. Press all seam allowances open.

4. Fuse the interfacing to wrong side of pink heart batik flap.

5. Place flap batting on work surface. Place striped flap over batting, right side up. Place pink heart batik flap over striped flap with right sides facing. Sew the side and bottom edges together, using a ½" seam allowance. Trim batting close to seam line. Trim remaining seam allowance to ¼". Clip seam allowance at curves to seam line. Edge-press the seam allowance open. Turn the flap right side out. Press.

6. Position one side of magnetic snap on batik side of flap ½" up from bottom edge and centered between sides.

sewing trim, flap, and front to back

1. Machine-baste edge of pom-pom fringe to upper edge of front, using a ½" seam allowance.

2. Sew the raw edge of flap to upper edge of front, right sides facing, using a ½" seam allowance. (See Illus. D)

Illus. D

3. Cut curve on bottom edges of front and back, using curved guideline from pattern A.

4. Sew front to back along side and bottom edges, right sides facing, using a ½" seam allowance. Clip seam allowance at curves to seam line but do not cut through stitches. Press seam allowance open. Turn right side out.

making inside flap pocket and sewing lining

1. Fold inside flat pocket poplin piece in half, right sides facing, aligning 10" edges. Machine-sew sides and bottom edges, leaving a 2" opening in the seam line along bottom edge. Clip bulk from the corners. Edge-press seam allowances open. Turn pocket right side out through bottom edge opening. Press flat.

2. Fuse interfacing to wrong side of one pink heart batik lining piece A.

3. Position pocket 1¼" upward from one 13" edge and centered between sides. Sew pocket to lining along sides and bottom edges. Sew pocket to lining along upper edge as well for a space of ½" from stitch line, then diagonally down to the side seam. *Note: This additional sewing on the pocket will keep the pocket from falling open inside the purse.*

inside flap and lining

4. Cut curve on bottom edges of both lining pieces A.

5. Sew lining front to back along sides and bottom edges, right sides facing, using a ½" seam allowance, leaving a 5" opening along bottom edge. Clip seam allowance at curves to seam line but do not cut through stitches. Press seam allowance open.

sewing lining to purse

1. Slip lining over purse, right sides facing, aligning top edges and matching side seams.

2. Sew lining to purse around top edges, using a ½" seam allowance. Press seam allowance toward outer purse fabric. (See Illus. E)

Illus. E

3. Turn right side out through opening in lining.

4. Slip lining inside purse and press top edge flat.

5. Topstitch around top edge with a decorative machine-embroidery stitch.

finishing

1. Working with 1½"-wide ribbon, mark 4" upward from both ends.

2. Fold ribbon length in half, aligning long edges, wrong sides facing. Using a very narrow zigzag stitch, machine-sew selvage edges together, sewing only between the 4" end marks.

3. Measure a 16" length on cord. Wrap masking tape around cord end and around 16" mark. Trim cord by cutting through middle of tape.

4. Pin and close safety pin through one cord end. Using pin, slip cord through one end of ribbon tube. When opposite cord end aligns with 4" mark on ribbon, stitch end of cord securely to ribbon at mark. Repeat with remaining cord end at opposite 4" mark on ribbon, forming the ribbon handle. remove safety pin.

5. Fold ends of ribbon over to overlap at center. Place ribbon ends on flap where indicated on pattern.

6. Sew ribbon ends to flap along sides and across flat ends. Sew upper ends with cord to flap. (See Illus. F)

Illus. F

7. Coat ribbon ends with fray preventative. When dry, trim with a diagonal slant.

8. Slip one end of ⅜"-wide ribbon through zipper pull. Fold ribbon in half and tie ends together. Coat ends with fray preventative. Trim ends at a slant when fray preventative has dried.

9. Position remaining side of magnetic snap on back so that it lines up with the snap on flap.

10. Sew button to door on front.

back view

sweet simplicity patterns

Enlarge patterns on this page 200% unless otherwise indicated.

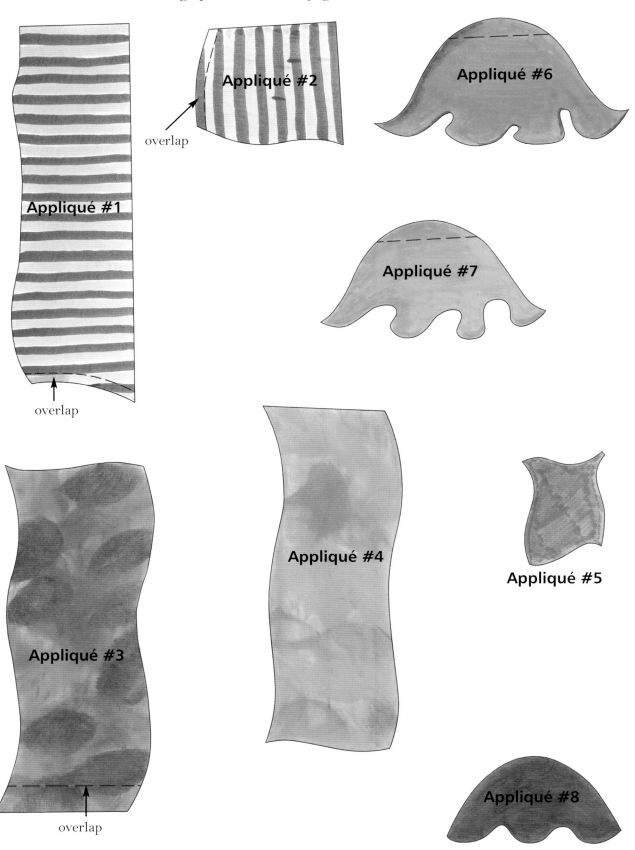

Appliqué #1

Appliqué #2

overlap

Appliqué #6

Appliqué #7

overlap

Appliqué #3

Appliqué #4

Appliqué #5

Appliqué #8

overlap

sweet simplicity patterns
Enlarge patterns on this page as indicated.

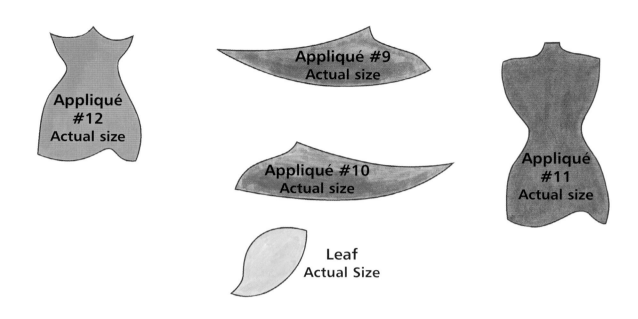

Appliqué #9
Actual size

Appliqué #12
Actual size

Appliqué #10
Actual size

Appliqué #11
Actual size

Leaf
Actual Size

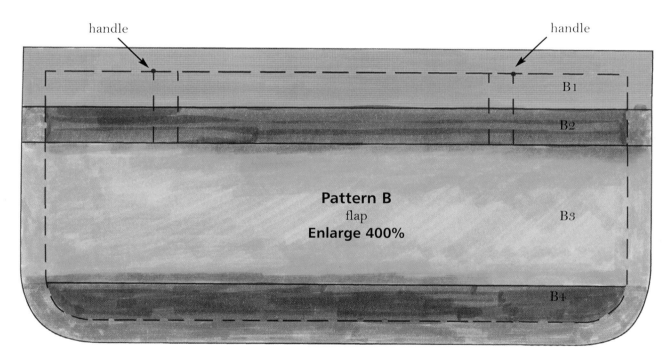

handle   handle

B1

B2

Pattern B
flap
Enlarge 400%

B3

B4

sweet simplicity pattern

Enlarge pattern on this page 200%.

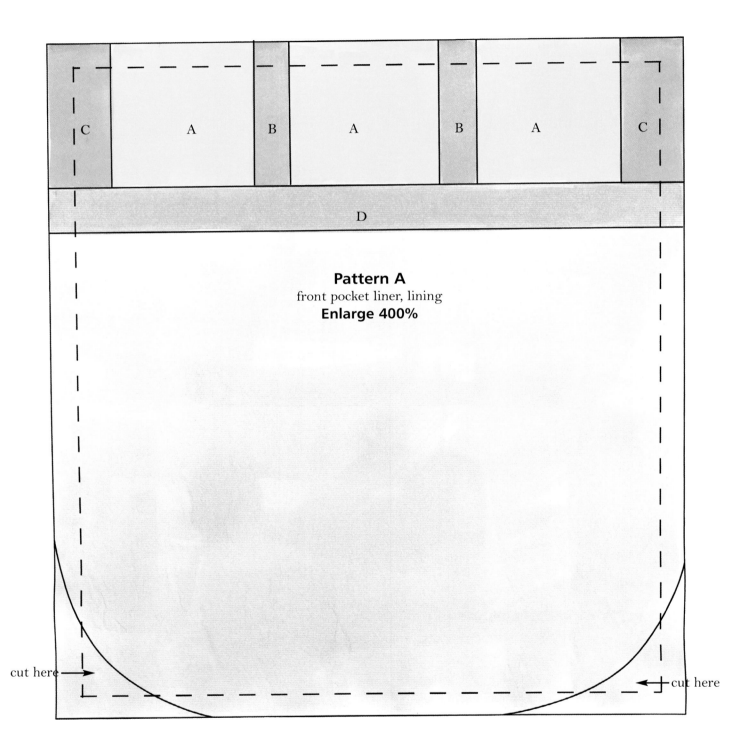

C   A   B   A   B   A   C

D

Pattern A
front pocket liner, lining
Enlarge 400%

cut here →   ← cut here

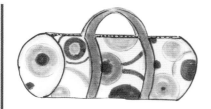

innocent optimism

To purely or untaintedly anticipate the best possible outcome or event.

Innocent Optimism photo shown on page 86

finished size
• 13" x 6½"

cotton fabrics

Aqua (2 variations)
• Aqua patterned (6" x 18") for circles D, E, F, G
• 44"-wide light aqua floral (⅜ yd) for Pattern A lining; Pattern B lining; bias; circles E, H, I

Brown (2 variations)
• Brown floral (6" x 13") for circles E, F, Pattern K
• Brown pin dot (6" x 13") for circles D, J

Ivory (2 variation)
• 44"-wide fusible fleece (½ yd) for Pattern A, Pattern B
• 54"-wide ribbed chenille (½ yd) for Pattern A; Pattern B

embellishments
• ⅛"-wide bright aqua ribbon (8")
• ⅛"-wide brown cotton piping (package)
• 1"-wide brown webbing (2 yds)
• 1"-wide single-fold brown bias tape

notions
• 14"–18" heavy-weight cream nylon zipper
• 22"-wide fusible woven interfacing (⅝ yd) for Pattern A; Pattern B; Pattern K
• Matching threads

tools
• General Tools on page 5
• Circle template
• Hand-sewing needle
• Quilter's freezer paper

cutting purse fabrics

Note: Enlarge Innocent Optimism Patterns on page 87 as indicated.

1. Using Pattern A, cut one body from ivory ribbed chenille fabric. Cut one body lining from light aqua floral fabric. Cut one from fusible interfacing. Cut one from fusible fleece that does not have seam allowance added. *Note: This is done to help eliminate bulk.*

2. Using Pattern B, cut two ends from ivory ribbed chenille fabric. Cut two end lining pieces from light aqua floral fabric. Cut two from fusible interfacing. Cut two from fusible fleece that do not have seam allowances added.

3. Cut 1"-wide bias strips from light aqua floral for a total length of 34" (piece as necessary) for outlined 10" circle C shape.

4. Using Pattern K, cut two tab pieces each from brown floral and fusible interfacing.

5. Using water-soluble fabric-marking pen, mark all fabric pieces as indicated with the patterns assembly markings. Refer to pattern pieces when assembling each bag.

cutting and preparing applique circles

1. Using the measurements for circles D–J on Appliqué Circle Chart on page 84 and mark circles D–J onto freezer paper. Cut out circles from paper.

2. Referring to Appliqué Circle Chart, prepare circles for appliqué from fabrics, following Steps 3–4 below.

3. For each circle press shiny side of freezer paper face downward onto wrong side of fabric. Trim circle away from fabric, adding a ¼" seam allowance all around when trimming.

4. Spray some starch into lid or small container. Saturate cotton swab with spray starch. Dab outer edge of fabric with swab. Clip outer edge of fabric up to freezer paper. Using iron on steam, press outer edges of fabric up over edge of freezer paper, being careful to maintain the circular shape. Remove freezer paper and press again.

appliqué circle chart		
pattern	cut quantity	fabric
D (5" circle)	3 altogether	Brown polka-dot (2) Aqua patterned (1)
E (4¼" circle)	6 altogether	Brown floral (1) Aqua patterned (2) Light aqua floral (3)
F (3" circle)	4 altogether	Brown floral (3) Aqua patterned (1)
G (2" circle)	3 altogether	Aqua patterned (3)
H (1¾" circle)	1 altogether	Light aqua floral (1)
I (1¼" circle)	2 altogether	Light aqua floral (2)
J (1" circle)	1 altogether	Brown polka-dot (1)

appliquéing bias onto 10" circle shapes

1. Make a 10" circle pattern from paper. Trace 10" circle onto right side of ivory ribbed chenille body fabric piece A where indicated on pattern. Two tracings are portions of circle. *Note: One tracing is a full circle.*

2. Fuse fleece to wrong side of body.

3. Working with brown bias tape, align raw edges of tape along traced line of one circle portion.

4. Working from fabric right side, machine-sew tape around circle, using a ¼" seam allowance on bias tape. (See Illus. A)

Illus. A

5. Trim bias tape seam allowance to a scant ⅛".

6. Fold and press finished edge of bias tape over seam allowance, enclosing it. Sew along finished edge of bias tape through all layers. (See Illus. B)

Illus. B

7. Repeat Steps 3–6 for the remaining traced circle portion.

8. Seam together light aqua floral bias strips as needed. Press strip in half, aligning long edges.

9. Sew strip to traced full circle by following Steps 3–6, overlapping edges when they meet. Begin and end sewing at outer side seam edge.

machine-appliquéing circles

1. Pin prepared circle appliqués onto right side of body where indicated on pattern.

2. Machine-sew each circle appliqué in place along outer finished edges. Press.

3. Fuse fleece to wrong sides of ivory ribbed chenille end pieces B.

4. Pin prepared circle appliqués onto right side of ends where indicated on pattern.

5. Sew circle appliqués in place. Press.

sewing handles onto body

1. Using water-soluble fabric-marking pen, mark handle placement onto right side of body where indicated on pattern.

2. Beginning at bottom center fold line on left handle side, pin webbing to body, allowing a ½" excess at starting point.

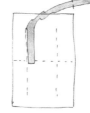

Illus. C

3. At upper mark, measure 15" on brown webbing. Place a pin at 15" measurement. (See Illus. C)

4. Begin pinning brown webbing to right handle side at 15" measurement mark. Extend and pin webbing to entire right handle side.

5. At right handle side lower mark, measure 15" on brown webbing. Place a pin at 15" measurement. (See Illus. D)

Illus. D

6. Complete pinning brown webbing to left handle side beginning with 15" measurement mark from Step 5.

7. At the original starting point, trim webbing with a ½" allowance.

8. Turn allowance under ½" to wrong side. Pin overlap in place

9. Machine-sew webbing to body along handle placement marks on both edges of webbing and across upper and lower marks. (See Illus. E)

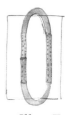

Illus. E

layering body with lining and sewing piping in place

1. Fuse interfacing to wrong side of light aqua floral body lining piece A.

2. Layer body piece and body lining piece, with wrong sides facing.

3. Pin and machine-baste outer edges together.

4. Sew right side of piping to right and left sides of layered body along long side edges, using a ½" seam allowance.

5. Along left side edge, break stitches 1¼" from top and bottom edges to allow for zipper. (See Illus. F)

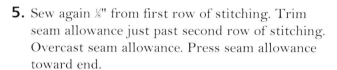

side view

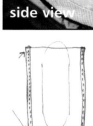

Illus. F

sewing zipper in place and making tab

1. Press the front and back top edges under ¾" to wrong side.

2. Beginning at left side, pin pressed-under edge to left edge of zipper tape, aligning pressed edge to edge of zipper coil. Using a zipper foot, machine-sew pressed edge to zipper tape. Trim seam allowance to ¼".

3. Sew again ⅜" from first row of stitching, catching in edge of zipper tape when sewing.

4. Repeat Steps 2–4 with opposite side of the zipper tape.

5. Fuse interfacing to wrong sides of tab pieces K.

6. Place tabs with right sides facing. Sew sides and curved edges together, using a ¼" seam allowance. Clip seam allowance to seam line. Edge-press seam allowance open. Turn right side out. Press.

7. With zipper closed, pin straight edge of tab to right edge of body at zipper. Machine-baste tab to right edge of body, being careful to not sew into zipper coil.

sewing ends to body

1. Make certain to have quarter marks on body and ends visible by remarking, if necessary, with water-soluble marking pen.

2. Clip body along side edges to seam line.

3. Pin one end to left body side, right sides facing, matching quarter marks.

4. Working from body side, sew end to body, using a ½" seam allowance.

5. Sew again ⅛" from first row of stitching. Trim seam allowance just past second row of stitching. Overcast seam allowance. Press seam allowance toward end.

6. Repeat Steps 3–5 for remaining end and right body side, being careful to not sew through the zipper coil.

finishing

1. At left zipper end, hand-stitch piping ends together so that piping completes the full end circle shape of bag.

zipper pull

2. Slip one end of ribbon through the zipper pull. Fold ribbon in half and tie the ends together. Coat ends with fray preventative.

3. Trim the ends at a slant when fray preventative has dried.

innocent optimism patterns

Enlarge patterns on this page as indicated.

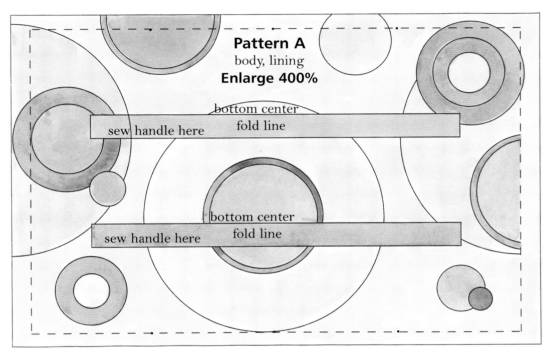

Pattern A
body, lining
Enlarge 400%

bottom center
fold line

sew handle here

bottom center
fold line

sew handle here

Note: The very largest circles are "outlined" with bias pieces.

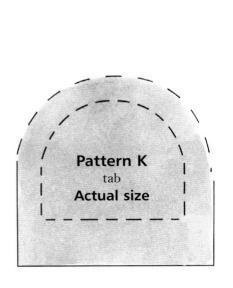

Pattern K
tab
Actual size

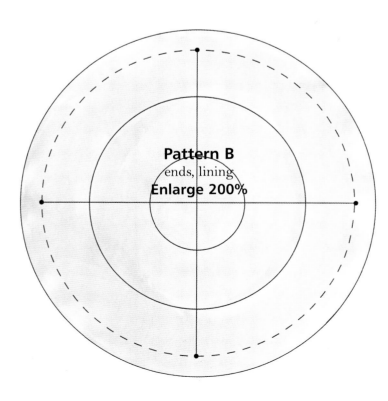

Pattern B
ends, lining
Enlarge 200%

romance

An emotional attraction or aura belonging to an heroic era, adventure, or activity.

finished size
- small 8" x 5"
- medium 10½" x 7"
- large 13" x 9"

cotton fabrics
- White quilted (18" x 9") for Pattern A small purse
- White quilted (23" x 10") for Pattern B medium purse
- White quilted (28" x 12½") for Pattern C large purse

embellishments
- ½"-wide ivory lettuce-edged trim (⅝ yd)
- 3½"-wide vintage embroidered eyelet (¼ yd) for small purse
- 12" sq. vintage embroidered hanky for medium and large purses

notions
- 9" off-white zipper for small purse
- 12" off-white zipper for medium purse
- 14"–16" off-white zipper for large purse
- White thread

tools
- General Tools on page 5
- Hand-sewing needle

cutting fabrics

Note: Enlarge Romance Patterns on pages 90–91 200% unless otherwise indicated.

1. Using Pattern A, cut two front/back pieces from white quilted cotton fabric for the small purse.

2. Using Pattern B, cut two front/back pieces from white quilted cotton fabric for medium purse.

3. Using Pattern C, cut two front/back pieces from white quilted cotton fabric for large purse.

4. Using water-soluble fabric-marking pen, mark all fabric pieces as indicated with the patterns assembly markings. Refer to pattern pieces when assembling each purse.

embellishing purse front

1. Machine-sew eyelet trim to right side of small front along top, sides, and bottom edges, placing unfinished edge of trim along top edge of front. Press.

2. For medium and large purses, position hanky corner centered on medium or large front. Sew hanky to front along top, sides, and corner edges. Trim excess hanky from sides and top edge of front. Press.

putting in zipper

1. Using water-soluble fabric-marking pen, mark fold line on front and back where indicated on pattern (1" from the top edges).

2. Sew top raw edges under ¼" to wrong side.

3. Press top edges under along the fold line.

4. Pin pressed-under edge of front to left edge of zipper tape, aligning fabric edge to edge of zipper coil, beginning with

Continued on page 90.

Continued from page 88.

zipper top stop at seam line. Using a zipper foot, sew front pressed edge to zipper tape. Sew again ⅛" from first row of stitching.

5. Align and sew back pressed edge to opposite side of zipper tape in the same manner.

6. Sew a new zipper end stop at seam line. With needle and quadrupled thread, stitch around zipper coil at seam line multiple times. Trim any excess zipper 1" past new end stop.

sewing front to back

1. Pin front and back together, right sides facing, aligning side and bottom edges.

2. Machine-sew side and bottom edges, avoiding dished-out corners at this time, using a ¼" seam allowance.

3. Overcast seam allowance.

4. Press side seam allowances toward back. Press bottom seam allowance toward front.

5. To make corners, fold one end from bottom seam line so that it meets end of adjacent side seam, with right sides facing. Pin in place. Repeat for remaining ends.

6. Sew across corners, using a ¼" seam allowance. Press seam allowances.

7. Turn right side out. Push out all corners.

finishing

1. At zipper top stop end, sew front and back zipper tapes together just to right of top stop metal pieces for a space of ⅛", hiding visibility of the seam allowance.

2. Slip one end of lettuce-edged trim through zipper pull. Fold trim in half and tie ends together. Coat ends with fray preventative. Trim ends at a slant when fray preventative has dried.

romance pattern

Enlarge pattern on this page 200%.

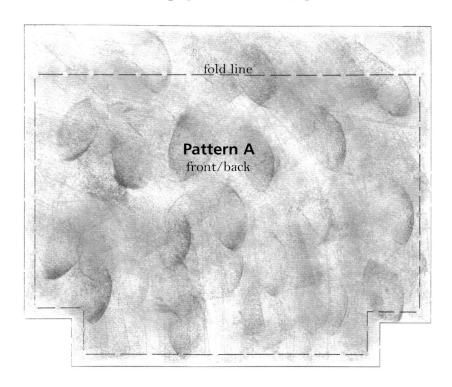

fold line

Pattern A
front/back

romance patterns

Enlarge patterns on this page 200%.

Note: Pattern B and Pattern C are stacked.

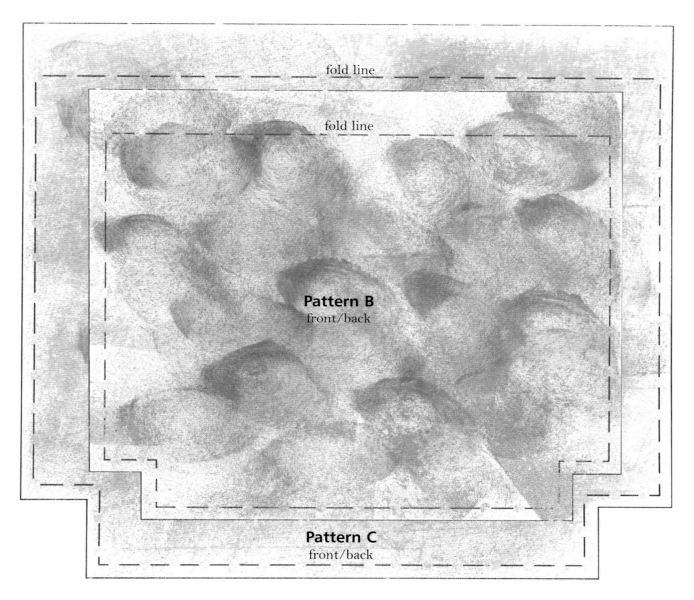

fold line

fold line

Pattern B
front/back

Pattern C
front/back

escape

To get away, to run wild from cultivation. To take a mental or an emotional break from the pressures of everyday life.

finished size
• 14" x 8", side gusset 3½"

cotton fabrics

Brown (1 variation)
• 44"-wide brown print barkcloth (½ yd) for Pattern A; Pattern B

Green (2 variations)
• 44"-wide green polka-dot print (¾ yd) for Pattern A lining; Pattern D; Pattern E lining; Pattern F
• 44"-wide green print barkcloth (⅜ yd) for Pattern B lining; Pattern C; Pattern E

embellishments
• ⅜" decorative black snap fasteners (2)
• ⅜"-wide ivory grosgrain ribbon (6")
• 1"-wide ivory ribbon with black checkered edges (4¼ yds)

notions
• ½"-wide self-adhesive black Velcro dots (2)
• 18" olive green nylon zipper
• 22"-wide medium-weight fusible woven interfacing (½ yd)
• 44"-wide cotton batting (⅜ yd)
• Matching threads

tools
• General Tools on page 5
• Hand-sewing needle

cutting tote fabrics

Note: Enlarge Escape Patterns on pages 96–97 200% unless otherwise indicated.

1. Using Pattern A, cut two front/back pieces from brown print barkcloth. Cut two from green polka-dot fabric for lining. Cut two from cotton batting.

2. Using Pattern B for front/back pocket, cut two from brown print barkcloth. Cut two from green print barkcloth for lining. Cut two from cotton batting.

3. Using Pattern C for patch pocket, cut two from green print barkcloth and two from fusible interfacing.

4. Using Pattern D for patch pocket flap, cut four from green polka-dot fabric. Cut two from fusible interfacing.

5. Using Pattern E for side gusset, cut one from green print barkcloth. Cut one from green polka-dot fabric for lining. Cut one from cotton batting.

6. Using Pattern F for zipper strips, cut two from green polka-dot fabric. Cut two from fusible interfacing.

7. Using water-soluble fabric-marking pen, mark all fabric pieces as indicated with the patterns assembly markings. Refer to pattern pieces when assembling each purse.

quilting tote front and back

1. Sandwich batting between the brown print front A and green polka-dot fabric lining front A, with wrong sides facing. Repeat for the backs A.

2. Using a free-motion machine-quilting technique, machine-quilt the front and the back.

3. For handles, cut two 30" lengths from 1"-wide ribbon. Cut two 17" lengths from ribbon. Cut two 17" x ¾" strips from fusible interfacing. Fuse interfacing to back side of the 17" lengths.

Continued on page 94.

Continued from page 92.

4. Pin one interfaced ribbon piece centered over one 30" ribbon piece. Sew the ribbons together along the selvage edges. Repeat with the remaining ribbon pieces.

5. Working with front, pin and sew one ribbon handle to front along handle placement lines indicated on Pattern A, leaving center portion of handle unsewn. (See Illus. A)

Illus. A

6. Repeat cutting tote fabrics Step 4–5 for back and other ribbon handle.

making front and back pockets

1. Pin front pocket batting to wrong side of brown print front pocket B. Place green print front pocket B lining piece over brown print pocket, right sides facing. Sew upper edges together, using a ½" seam allowance. Trim batting close to seam line. Press seam allowance toward brown print. Fold lining to back side along seam line. Press. (See Illus. B)

Illus. B

2. Repeat Step 1 for remaining pocket pieces.

3. Using a free-motion machine-quilting technique, machine-quilt front pockets.

making patch pockets

1. Fuse interfacing to wrong side of patch pocket C pieces.

2. Fold patch pockets in half along fold line indicated on pattern. Sew sides and bottom edges together, using a ¼" seam allowance, leaving small opening along seam line on one side. Trim bulk from corners. Edge-press seam allowance open. Turn right side out through seam line opening. Press.

3. Sew patch pockets to front pocket along sides and bottom edges where indicated on pattern B. (See Illus. C)

Illus. C

4. Fuse interfacing to two patch pocket flap D pieces.

5. Sew ribbon trim to interfaced flaps. (See Illus. D)

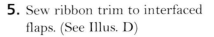

Illus. D

6. Pin one remaining flap to a trimmed flap with right sides facing. Sew sides and bottom edges together, using a ¼" seam allowance. Repeat for remaining flap pieces.

7. Pin straight edge of one flap to front pocket upward along pocket flap placement line, with right sides facing, allowing for a ½" seam allowance. (See Illus. E)

Illus. E

8. Sew flap to front pocket on placement line. Turn flap raw edges under ¼", then topstitch close to turned-under edge for a clean finish. Press flap downward. *Note: The patch pockets are on the front pocket only.*

9. Layer front and back pockets onto front and back pieces. Machine-baste layers together along side and bottom edges. Topstitch center of pockets to center of front and back pieces.

making side gusset

1. Sandwich batting between green print side gusset E and green polka-dot lining side gusset E, with wrong sides facing.

2. Using a free-motion machine-quilting technique, machine-quilt the side gusset. Fuse the interfacing pieces to the wrong side of the zipper strips F. Press the strips in half, aligning the long edges.

3. Pin folded edge of one zipper strip to left edge of zipper tape, aligning fabric edge to edge of zipper coil. Using a zipper foot, machine-sew folded edge to zipper tape. Sew again ⅛" from first row of stitching.

4. Align and sew edge of other zipper strip to opposite side of the zipper tape in the same manner as with Step 3.

5. Sew the ribbon trim onto zipper strips next to zipper coil.

6. Cut 3" length from ribbon. Fold ribbon in half, aligning ends and forming a loop.

7. With zipper closed, pin ends of loop centered onto right end of zipper strips, with right sides facing. (See Illus. F) Baste-stitch in place.

Illus. F

8. Sew side gusset to zipper strips at short ends. Press seam allowances toward side gusset.

9. Topstitch seam allowance ¼" from seam line onto side gusset.

sewing gusset to front and back

1. Pin and sew side gusset/zipper strips to tote front with right sides facing, matching center-front top edge and bottom edge dots and using a ½" seam allowance. Work from side gusset/zipper strips side when sewing. Clip side gusset/zipper strips to seam line along curved edges of tote front. Press seam allowance toward side gusset/zipper strips. (See Illus. G)

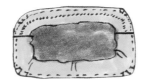

Illus. G

2. Sew again ¼" from first row of stitching. Trim seam allowance just past second row of stitching. Overcast seam allowance.

3. Repeat Steps 1–2 for purse back.

4. Working from outside of purse, fold front along front/side gusset and zipper strip seam line.

5. Topstitch around front close to seam line. Repeat for the back. *Note: This step will help to keep the purse shape defined.*

finishing

1. Apply the snap fasteners to the flaps, following manufacturer's directions. If flap is too thick, apply snap front piece only. Position Velcro dots on back side of flap and on patch pocket.

step 1

2. Slip ribbon through zipper pull. Tie ribbon ends together. Coat ends with fray preventative. When dry, trim ends at a slant.

zipper pull

back view

escape patterns

Enlarge patterns on this page 200% unless otherwise indicated.

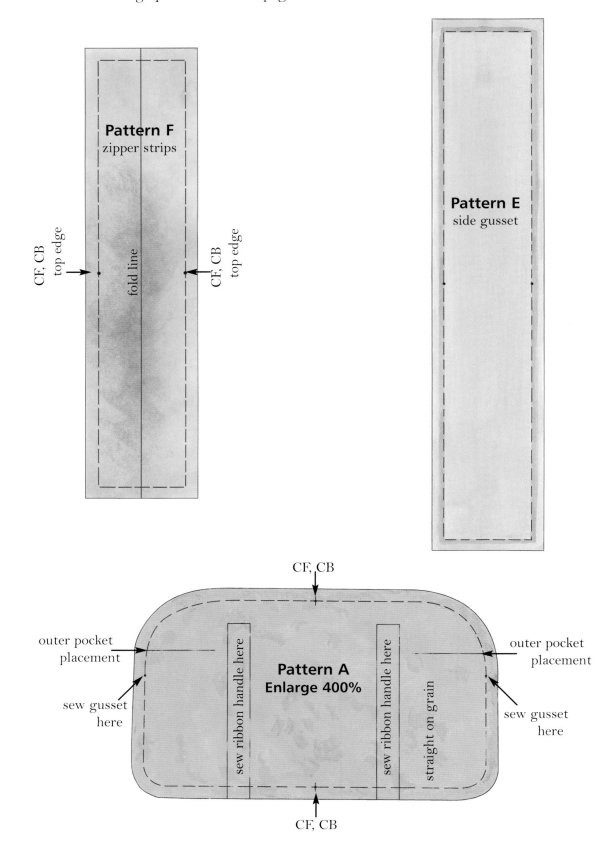

Pattern F
zipper strips

CF, CB
top edge

fold line

CF, CB
top edge

Pattern E
side gusset

CF, CB

outer pocket
placement

sew gusset
here

sew ribbon handle here

Pattern A
Enlarge 400%

sew ribbon handle here

straight on grain

outer pocket
placement

sew gusset
here

CF, CB

escape patterns

Enlarge patterns on this page 200%.

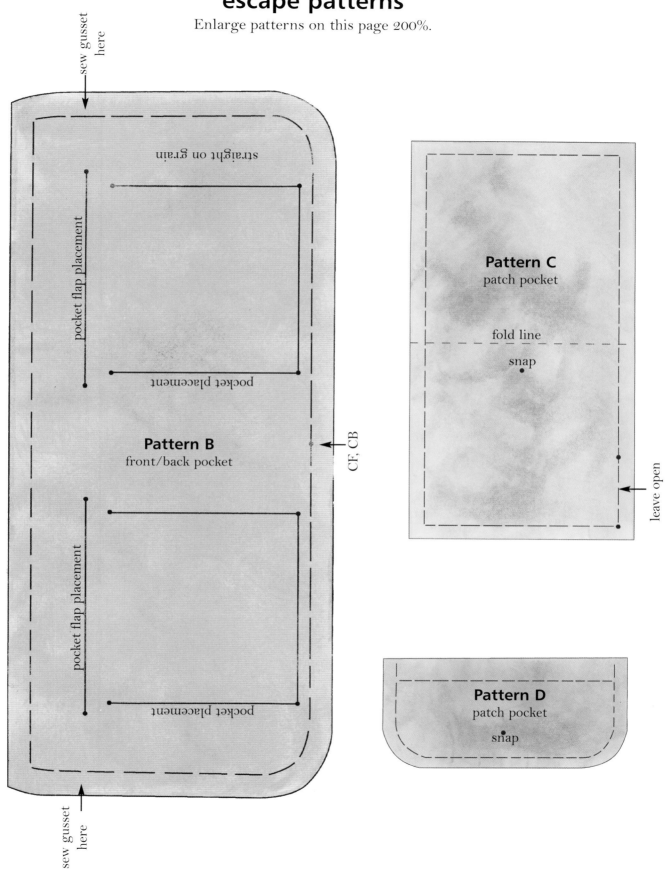

sew gusset here

straight on grain

pocket flap placement

pocket placement

Pattern B
front/back pocket

CF, CB

pocket flap placement

pocket placement

sew gusset here

Pattern C
patch pocket

fold line

snap

leave open

Pattern D
patch pocket

snap

sense of balance

The ability to bring into harmony or proportion. Mental and emotional steadiness.

finished size
• 15" x 6½", 5" at sides

embellishments
• ½"-wide red cotton ribbon (6")
• 1"-wide rectangle rings (4)
• Red suede rose

embroidery
• 4mm silk ribbons: forest green, sage green
• 7mm red silk ribbon
• 13mm dark red silk ribbon
• ½"-wide vintage bobbin lace (¼ yd)
• 4" dia. natural white vintage linen doily
• Embroidery flosses: medium green; olive; red; rusty rose

fabrics
Cream (1 variation)
• Cream moire (4" x 5")
Olive Green (1 variation)
• 44"-wide olive print cotton (½ yd) for lining/backing
Peach (4 variations)
• Four different muted peach print cotton (¼ yd each) for tote body
Red/cream (2 variations)
• 44"–54"-wide red/cream plaid cotton (⅛ yd) for tote upper strips
• 44"-wide red/cream patterned cotton corduroy (⅛ yd) for Pattern B; handle; body trim
• 44"–54"-wide embroidered linen (¼ yd) for Pattern A
• 44"–54"-wide small floral linen (¼ yd) for outer pockets
Tan (3 variations)
• Three different tan cotton prints (¼ yd each) for tote body

notions
• 16" ecru zipper
• 44"-wide cotton batting (½ yd)
• Matching threads

tools
• General Tools on page 5
• Large safety pin
• Needles: darning; embroidery size 3; hand-sewing

sewing "trip around the world" piece for tote body

1. Using grid-lined ruler, cut three 1⅜" x 44" strips from muted peach cotton fabrics and three 1⅜" x 44" strips from tan cotton fabric.

2. Place three strips cut from each cotton fabric in piles, arranging the fabrics next to each other as desired.

3. Pick up one strip each from first two piles. Align long edges and place strips with right sides facing. Sew strips together along one long edge. Press seam allowance toward one side.

4. Pick up one strip each from third and fourth piles. Sew together as in Step 3.

5. Pick up one strip each from the fifth and sixth piles. Sew together as in Step 3. Pick-up one strip from seventh pile. Sew to the sixth strip.

6. Sew strips from Steps 3–4 together. Continue to press seam allowances toward same side.

7. Sew strips from Steps 5–6 together. Press seam allowances toward same side.

8. Repeat Steps 3–7 with remaining sets of strips. Press seam allowances toward the same side.

9. Sew three-striped sets together, forming a piece of horizontally striped fabric. Press seam allowances toward same side.

Continued on page 100.

Continued from page 98.

10. Mist striped fabric with water-filled spray bottle and press well from the right side.

11. Using grid-lined ruler, cut the horizontally striped fabric into 1⅜"-wide vertical strips.

12. With fabrics matching in direction, align two strips along one long edge, with right sides facing. Lift the top strip and move it down one square. Sew strips together along one long edge, matching the seam lines, but keeping fabrics offset by one square.

13. Repeat Step 12 for each vertical strip.

14. Sew sets of vertical strips together, continuing to offset fabrics by one square.

15. Press seam allowance toward same side. Mist with water-filled bottle and press well from right side. *Note: This completed Trip Around the World piece will have the shape of a parallelogram.*

cutting fabrics

Note: Enlarge Sense of Balance Patterns on page 102 200% unless otherwise indicated.

1. Using Pattern A for tote side, cut two from embroidered linen and two from olive print fabric.

2. Using Pattern B for tabs, cut two from red/cream patterned corduroy. Cut two handles 20" x 2" from red/cream patterned corduroy. Cut one handle trim piece 10" x 2" from red/cream patterned corduroy. Cut two body trim pieces 22" x 2" from red/cream patterned corduroy.

3. From the Trip Around the World piece, cut one tote body 17" x 19", so that squares are placed on point across the width and length.

4. Cut two tote upper strips 17" x 3¾" from red/cream plaid.

5. Cut four pockets 8" square from the small floral linen.

6. Cut one lining/backing piece 27" x 17" from the olive print and one from the cotton batting.

7. Using water-soluble fabric-marking pen, mark all fabric pieces as indicated with the patterns assembly markings. Refer to pattern pieces when assembling each tote.

embroidering one pocket

1. Using Pattern C for embroidered heart, cut one from cream moiré. Place heart centered on pocket.

embroidered pocket

2. Cut linen doily in half. Position doily halves underneath upper-left and lower-right sides of heart. Pin in place

3. Pin straight edge of piece of lace underneath right and lower-left sides of heart.

4. Hand-stitch doily halves, moiré heart, and lace trim in place.

5. Using pencil, transfer lettering and stem elements from Stitch Transfer on page 102 to heart/doily halves. Embroider design as follows:

a. Using Outline Stitch on page 9, embroider lettering with two strands of the rusty rose floss.

b. Using Outline Stitch, embroider stems with three strands of olive or medium green floss.

c. Using Couching Stitch on page 9, embroider wavy line along right side of heart with three strands of medium green floss, then couched by three strands of olive floss.

d. Using darning needle and Lazy Daisy Stitch on page 9, embroider center of large roses and rosebuds with 13mm dark red silk ribbon. Using ribbon stitch, form larger petals.

e. Using Lazy Daisy Stitch, embroider center of smaller roses and rosebuds with 7mm red silk ribbon.

f. Using Ribbon Stitch on page 9, form larger petals.

g. Using Bullion Lazy Daisy Stitch on page 9, embroider leaves with 4mm forest green and sage green silk ribbon. Using ribbon stitch, form rose calyxes.

h. Using French Knot on page 9, embroider tiny rosebuds with three strands of red floss.

i. Using Lazy Daisy Stitch, embroider tiny leaves near tiny rosebuds with two strands of medium green floss.

j. Using Buttonhole Stitch on page 9, embroider upper-left edge of heart with two strands of olive floss.

sewing and quilting tote body

1. Sew tote upper strips to front and back top edges of tote body, right sides facing, aligning 17" edges, using a ¼" seam allowance. Press seam allowance toward upper strips.

2. Place olive print lining (backing) piece on work surface, wrong side up. Place batting piece over it. Position pieced body over batting, right side up. Pin layers together.

3. Using a free-motion machine-quilting technique, machine-quilt layers together. Trim quilted piece 16" x 25½".

4. Fold body in half, aligning front and back top edges, to find center bottom of body. Using water-soluble fabric-marking pen, mark center bottom along fold on both side edges. Measure and mark 2¾" from either side of center mark along two side edges. *Note: These marks will match up to the bottom corners of the tote side pieces A.* Measure and mark 7⅛" from either side of the bottom corner marks. *Note: These marks will match up to the top corners of the tote side pieces A.*

making and applying pockets

1. Place embroidered pocket with another pocket piece, right sides facing. Sew upper and lower edges, using a ¼" seam allowance. Turn right side out. Press. Repeat with other two pocket pieces.

2. Position pockets centered on quilted body, aligning top edge of each pocket with tote upper strip/tote body seam lines. Pin in place.

3. Sew pockets to body along pocket bottom edge. Sew sides of pockets to body, using a ⅛" seam allowance.

trimming pockets

1. Fold one body trim piece in half, right sides facing. Trim piece in half, right sides facing, aligning the long edges. Sew the long edges together, using a ¼" seam allowance. Turn body trim piece right side out. Center seam line and press body trim piece flat. Repeat with the second body trim piece.

2. Wrap ends of each trim piece over one bar of rectangle rings. Pin wrap-over in place.

3. Position trim pieces along side edges of pockets, extending trim up onto tote upper strips. Sew trim pieces to body along both edges and across wrapped-over ends.

applying zipper

1. Press top and bottom edges of body under ⅜" to wrong side.

2. Pin pressed-under top edge of body to left edge of zipper tape, aligning fabric edge to edge of zipper coil. Using a zipper foot, machine-sew pressed edge of body to zipper tape. Align and sew opposite pressed-under edge of the body to opposite side of zipper tape in the same manner. *Note: The body now has a tube shape.*

side view

3. Place two tabs with right sides facing. Sew sides and curved edge, using a ¼" seam allowance. Turn tab right side out.

4. Pin raw edge of tab centered to body side at end of zipper.

sewing sides to body

1. Layer embroidered linen and olive print tote side pieces A together, with wrong sides facing.

2. Pin and sew duffel side A to body sides, with right sides facing, matching top and bottom corner marks, using a ½" seam allowance. Sew again ⅛" from first row of stitching. Trim seam allowance just past second row of stitching. Overcast seam allowance. Press seam allowance toward sides.

making handle

1. Press long edges of handle pieces under ¼" to fabric wrong side. Press in half, aligning pressed-under edges. Sew pressed-under edges together. Topstitch along other edge as well. Repeat with handle trim pieces.

2. Cut handle trim piece into four 2½" lengths. Fold one length in half, right sides facing. Sew across ends, using a ¼" seam allowance. Press seam

suede rose

allowance open. Turn right side out. Repeat with remaining trim pieces.

3. Slip each handle end through each trim piece.

4. Wrap ends of each handle over other bar of rectangle rings. Hand-stitch wrap-over in place. Slip handle trim pieces over raw edge from wrap-over. Stitch handle trim piece in place.

5. Attach suede rose to tote with a safety pin.

sense of balance patterns

Enlarge patterns on this page 200%.

center top

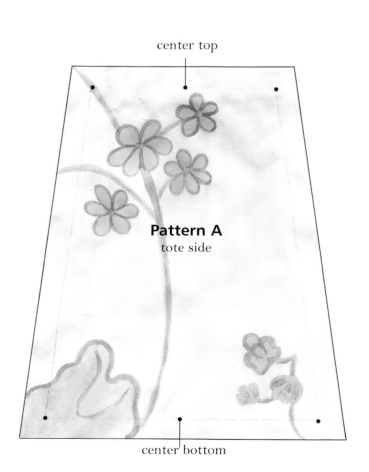

Pattern A
tote side

center bottom

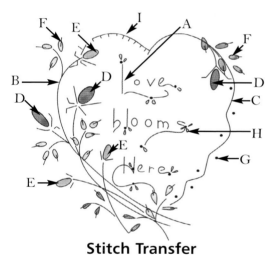

Stitch Transfer

Pattern B
tab

Pattern C
heart

outspokenness

Direct and open in speech or expression. Expressed without any reserve.

Outspokenness photo shown on page 105

finished size
• 7" x 12"

cotton fabrics
• 1¼"-wide–2¼"-wide x 15" scraps in any coloration for strip-piecing (30)
• 44"-wide yellow/blue striped (¼ yd) for A; C bottom narrow strip; E drawstring strip

Cream (2 variations)
• 23" x 1¼" cream/gray/rose small print for C middle narrow strip
• 44"-wide cream/brown small print (½ yd) for Pattern A; C middle narrow strip; F backing

embellishments
• ⅜"-wide gray/black striped ribbon (1 yd)

notions
• 44"-wide cotton batting (½ yd)
• Matching threads

tools
• General Tools on page 5
• Large safety pin
• Pinking shears

sewing strip scraps together
1. Using random fabrics and widths, sew approximately 30 scraps together, right sides facing, using a ¼" seam allowances, so that the pieced scraps measure 23" in width.
2. Press seam allowances toward one side.

cutting fabrics
Note: Enlarge Outspokenness Pattern on page 103 200% unless otherwise indicated.

1. From the pieced scraps, cut three 23" x 3½" pieces B and one 23" x 2" piece D.
2. Using Pattern A, cut one base each from the yellow/blue striped and cream/brown small print fabrics. Cut one from the cotton batting.
3. Cut one narrow strip each C 23" x 1¼" from yellow/blue striped, cream/brown small print, and cream/gray/rose small print fabrics.
4. Cut one drawstring strip E 23" x 2½" from yellow/blue striped fabric.
5. Cut one each 23" x 14½" backing/batting piece F from the cream/brown small print fabric and from the cotton batting.
6. Using water-soluble fabric-marking pen, mark all fabric pieces as indicated with the patterns assembly markings Refer to pattern pieces when assembling each tote.

sewing pieces to batting/backing
1. Place backing fabric on work surface, right side down. Layer the batting on top of the backing piece. Pin the layers together.
2. Position C strip yellow/blue striped piece along one edge of layered fabrics, aligning 23" edges. Pin in place.

3. Place one B strip over the C strip, right sides facing, aligning one 23" edge of B strip with upper edge of C strip. Sew strips together and to backing/batting, using a ¼" seam allowance. Flip B strip open. Press.

4. Sew C cream/brown small print strip to upper edge of B strip along 23" edges and to backing batting as in Step 3, using a ¼" seam allowance. Flip C strip open. Press.

5. Repeat Step 3.

6. Repeat Step 4, using cream/gray/rose small print B strip.

7. Repeat Step 3. Sew upper edge of strip to backing/batting.

8. Using disappearing ink pen, draw a line onto backing/batting piece that is ¼" above top edge of third B strip.

9. Position 2"-wide D strip along marked line. Sew bottom edge of D strip to backing/batting. Sew upper edge to backing/batting ½" from edge.

10. Using pinking shears, trim upper edge of D strip.

sewing drawstring strip

1. Press long edges of E drawstring strip under ¼" to wrong side. Press ends under ½" to wrong side. Press strip in half, aligning long edges.

2. Sew long edges of drawstring over space between upper B strip and the D strip, placing ends ½" from side edges. Do not sew across short ends.

finishing

1. Sew side edges together, wrong sides facing, using a ½" seam allowance, forming a cylinder shape.

2. Trim seam allowance edges with pinking shears.

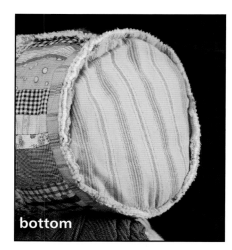

bottom

drawstring with ribbon

3. Fold cylinder in half. Mark bottom edge at half point. Fold cylinder in quarters and mark bottom edge at quarter points.

4. Place cream/brown print base on work surface, wrong side up. Place batting over this. Place yellow/blue strip base over batting, right side up. Pin layers together. Mark base at quarter points.

5. Pin cylinder to base, wrong sides facing, aligning quarter marks, half mark and side seam with base quarter points. Sew the cylinder to base, using a ½" seam allowance.

6. Trim base seam allowance with pinking shears.

7. Use safety pin to insert ribbon through drawstring. Tie ribbon ends together. Coat ends with fray preventative. Trim at a slant when dry.

outspokenness pattern
Enlarge pattern on this page 200%.

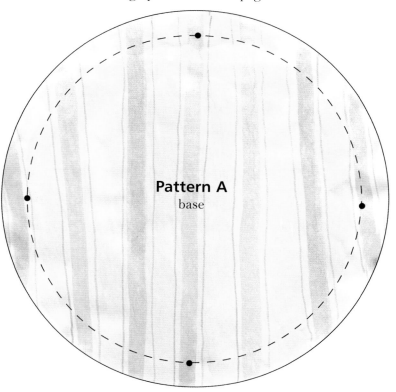

Pattern A
base

large purses

A bag or tote exceeding others in quantity or size.
Having more than the usual capacity.

heartfelt comfort

A deeply felt feeling or experience that gives or brings contentment.

Heartfelt Comfort photo shown on page 110

finished size
• 18" x 11", gusset 3½"

embellishments
• 1⅛" wooden button

fabrics
• 44"-wide fusible fleece (¼ yd) for Pattern D

Blue (3 variations)
• 44"-wide blue checkered cotton (¼ yd) for Pattern B
• 44"-wide blue print cotton (1 yd) for Pattern A lining; Pattern D; Pattern E lining; Pattern I lining
• 44"-wide blue striped cotton (¼ yd) for Pattern I

Brown (3 variations)
• 44"-wide brown checkered cotton (⅛ yd) for handle front J; Pattern G; zipper pull L
• 44"-wide brown print cotton (¼ yd) for Pattern C
• 54"–60"-wide fleece-backed brown faux suede (½ yd) for Patterns A, E, F, G, H; handle back K

notions
• ¾"-wide elastic (⅜ yd)
• 17"-wide iron-on vinyl (2½ yds) for Pattern A lining; Pattern D; Pattern E lining; Pattern I
• 24" gold-toothed metal zipper
• Matching threads

tools
• General Tools on page 5
• Large safety pin
• Needles: hand-sewing; jeans

cutting fabrics

Note: Enlarge Heartfelt Comfort Patterns on pages 111–113 200% unless otherwise indicated.

1. Using Pattern A, cut two for front and back from fleece-backed brown faux suede. Cut two each for front and back lining from blue cotton print and iron-on vinyl.

2. Using Pattern B, cut two for center outer pocket from blue cotton checkered fabric.

3. Using Pattern C, cut four for side outer pocket from brown cotton print.

4. Using Pattern D, cut two each for outer pocket lining from blue cotton print and iron-on vinyl. Cut two from fusible fleece that does not have ½" seam allowance added. *Note: This is done to help eliminate bulk.*

5. Using Pattern E, cut one for side gusset from fleece-backed brown faux suede. Cut one each for side gusset lining from blue cotton print and iron-on vinyl.

6. Using Pattern F, cut two for zipper strips from fleece-backed brown faux suede.

7. Using Pattern G, cut one each for tab from fleece-backed brown faux suede and brown cotton check.

8. Using Pattern H, cut one for flap from fleece-backed brown faux suede.

9. Using Pattern I, cut two each for side gusset pocket from blue striped, blue print and iron-on vinyl fabric.

10. Cut two handle pieces J 2" x 38" from brown cotton checkered fabric.

11. Cut two handle pieces K 2¼" x 38" from fleece-backed brown faux suede.

12. Cut one zipper pull piece L 9" x 1¼" from brown cotton checkered fabric.

13. Using water-soluble fabric-marking pen, mark all fabric pieces as indicated with the pattern assembly markings.

Refer to pattern pieces when assembling each bag. *Note: Seam allowances ½" unless otherwise noted.*

making outer pockets

1. Sew side outer pockets to center outer pockets along side edges, right sides facing. Press seam allowances open.

2. Fuse fusible fleece centered to wrong sides of assembled outer pockets.

3. Adhere iron-on vinyl to right sides of outer pocket lining pieces, following manufacturer's directions.

4. Pin outer pockets to pocket lining pieces, right sides facing. Sew upper edges together. Press seam allowance toward outer pocket. Fold lining to back side along seam line. Press.

5. Topstitch close to finished edge.

6. Using free-motion machine-quilting technique, machine-quilt the outer pockets.

7. Pin side and bottom edges of outer pockets to front and back faux suede pieces. *Note: The center pocket will be pleated at the side seam edges once the handles have been sewn in place.*

making handles

1. Working with handle front pieces J, press the long edges under ½" to fabric wrong side.

2. Working with handle back pieces K, pin long edges over ½" to faux suede side so that the fleeced edges are visible.

3. Pin wrong side of one handle front piece onto fleece-edged side of one handle back piece, centering handle front on handle back.

4. Sew handle layers together close to pressed-under edge of front along the long edges.

5. Repeat Steps 3–4 for other handle front and back pieces.

side gusset pocket

6. Pin and sew handles to outer pocket/front and outer pocket/back pieces along handle placement lines indicated on Pattern A.

7. Pleat excess from center outer pocket side edges toward handles. Pin in place.

8. Adhere iron-on vinyl to right sides of front and back lining pieces.

9. Pin front and back to the front and back lining pieces, with wrong sides facing. Machine-baste layered fronts along all edges, using a ⅜" seam allowance. Repeat with layered backs.

making flap

1. Working with flap piece H, machine-overcast side and curved edges.

2. Pin overcast edges over ½" to faux suede side so that a fleece edge is visible.

3. Topstitch ⅜" from outer edge.

4. Make a buttonhole on flap where indicated on the pattern.

5. Pin right side of flap centered to top edge of back. *Note: This is the suede side where the fleece edge is visible.* Machine-baste in place, using a ⅜" seam allowance.

making side gusset pockets

1. Adhere iron-on vinyl to right sides of side gusset pocket lining pieces.

2. Sew side gusset pocket pieces to side gusset pocket lining pieces along top and bottom edges, right sides facing. Press seam allowance toward outer fabric pieces.

3. Turn the pockets right side out. Press.

4. To make elastic casing, top-stitch pockets close to top edges. Topstitch again ½" from first row of stitching.

5. Cut elastic into two 5" lengths. Using safety pin,

slip elastic through casing. Make certain to machine-baste end of elastic to pocket side edge before exiting elastic through opposite end of casing. Baste-stitch elastic at opposite end to pocket side edge.

6. Pin vinyl side of side gusset pockets to suede side of side gusset where indicated on side gusset Pattern E.

7. Sew pockets to gusset along bottom edges. Machine-baste pockets to gusset along side edges.

making side gusset

1. Adhere iron-on vinyl to right sides of side gusset lining piece.

2. Place side gusset and side gusset lining piece together with wrong sides facing. Pin along outer edges. Machine-baste outer edges together, using a ⅜" seam allowance.

3. Working with zipper strip pieces F, machine-overcast one long edge from each piece.

4. Pin each overcast edge over ½" to faux suede side so that a fleece edge is visible.

front flap button

5. Pin folded edge of one zipper strip to left edge of zipper tape, aligning fabric edge to edge of zipper coil. Using a zipper foot, machine-sew folded edge to zipper tape. Sew again ⅜" from first row of stitching.

6. Align and sew edge of remaining zipper strip to opposite side of zipper tape in the same manner as with Step 5.

7. Place two tab pieces E with right sides facing. Sew side and curved edges, using a ¼" seam allowance. Clip seam allowance at curve to seam line. Edge-press seam allowance open. Turn right side out. Press.

8. With zipper closed, pin tab onto right end of zipper strips with right sides facing.

9. Sew side gusset to zipper strips at short ends, making certain to not catch elasticized edges of side gusset pockets into seam line when sewing. Press seam allowances open. Do not stitch through zipper teeth.

sewing gusset to front and back

1. Pin and sew side gusset/zipper strips to front with right sides facing, matching center front along top and bottom edges. Work from side gusset/zipper strips side when sewing. Clip side gusset/zipper strips to the seam line along curved edges of bag front when sewing.

2. Sew again ⅛" from first row of stitching. Trim seam allowance just past second row of stitching. Using a tight zigzag stitch, overcast seam allowance.

3. Repeat Steps 1–2 for bag back, making certain to open zipper a bit in order to turn bag right side out.

finishing

1. Hand-stitch a button to the center outer pocket front where indicated on the pattern.

2. Working with zipper pull piece L, press long edges under ¼" to wrong side.

3. Press in half, aligning pressed-under edges.

4. Machine-sew layers together along pressed-under edges.

5. Slip zipper-pull fabric piece through zipper pull. Sew layers together. Coat ends with fray preventative. When dry, cut ends at a slant.

6. Fold flap over onto front. Button closed.

heartfelt comfort patterns

Enlarge patterns on this page as indicated.

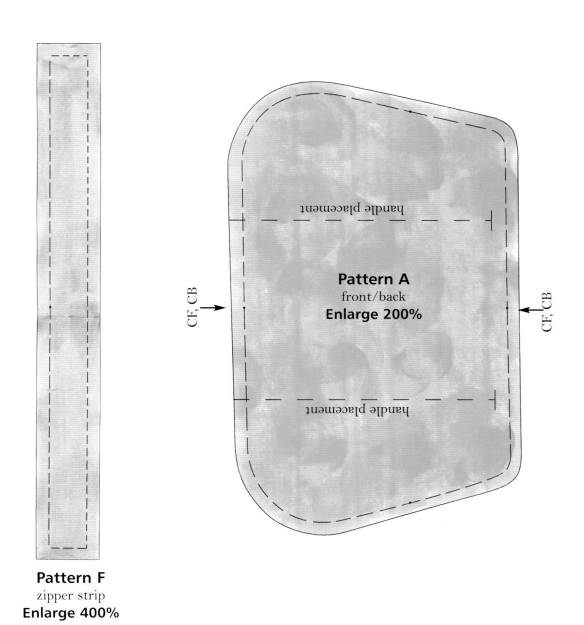

Pattern A
front/back
Enlarge 200%

handle placement

handle placement

CF, CB

CF, CB

Pattern F
zipper strip
Enlarge 400%

heartfelt comfort patterns

Enlarge patterns on this page 200%.

pin top edge of side pocket here

sew bottom edge of side pocket here

Pattern E
side gusset, lining

on fold

CF   CB

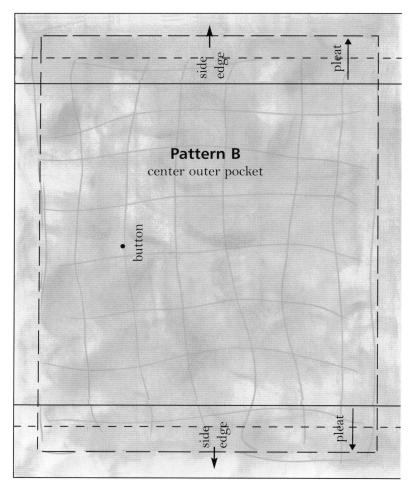

side edge

pleat

Pattern B
center outer pocket

button

side edge

pleat

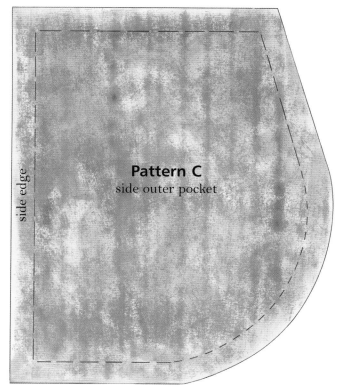

side edge

Pattern C
side outer pocket

heartfelt comfort pattern

Enlarge patterns on this page 200% unless otherwise indicated.

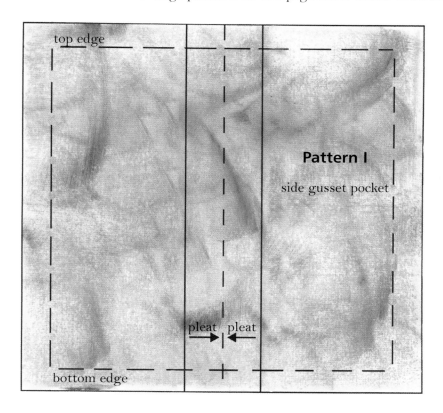

top edge

Pattern I

side gusset pocket

pleat | pleat

bottom edge

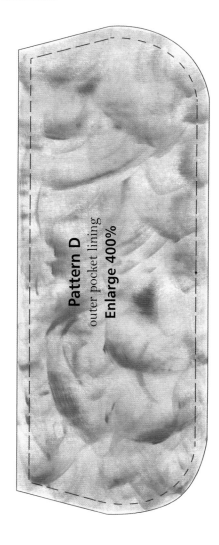

Pattern D
outer pocket lining
Enlarge 400%

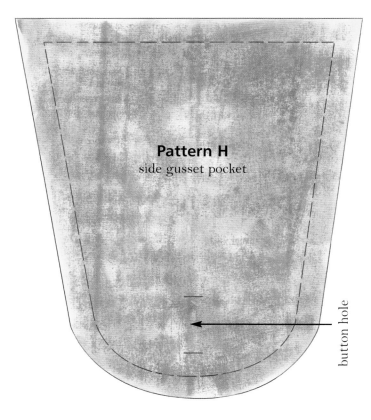

Pattern H
side gusset pocket

button hole

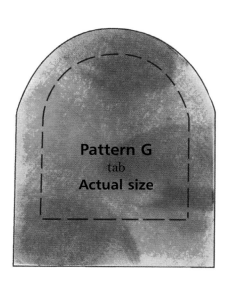

Pattern G
tab
Actual size

delight

To give keen enjoyment. To take great pleasure.

finished size
- 18½" x 12"

cotton fabrics
Cream (1 variation)
- Cream patterned (4½" x 9") for quilt block

Green (2 variation)
- Light green variegated (7" x 5") for quilt block
- Lime green/chartreuse purchased kitchen towel (20" x 29") for outer bag body

Yellow (8 variations)
- 44"-wide yellow/gray/white plaid (¼ yd) for handle E; handle wrap piece F; tab G
- Four different yellow prints (4" x 5" each) for quilt block
- Yellow-gold/orange purchased kitchen towel (20" x 29") for lining
- Yellow/orange patterned (2" x 4") for quilt block
- Yellow patterned (6½" sq.) for pocket lining C

embellishments
- ½"-wide yellow grosgrain ribbon (6")

notions
- 20" olive green zipper
- 22"-wide fusible woven interfacing (½ yd) for pocket lining C, handle E
- 22"-wide lightweight nonwoven interfacing (⅛ yd) for foundation-pieced quilt block
- 44"-wide cotton batting (½ yd)
- Matching threads

tools
- General Tools on page 5
- Fine-tipped brown permanent ink fabric-marking pen
- Hand-sewing needle

making foundation-pieced quilt block
Note: The pieces #7 and #7a, #8, and #8a are preseamed before sewing in place on the foundation.

Refer to Foundation Piecing on pages 7–8 before beginning.

1. Using Unit A pattern on page 117 for foundation-pieced quilt block, trace four of Unit A onto lightweight nonwoven interfacing, using permanent ink pen and grid-lined ruler. Be certain to add the seam allowance to each traced piece.

2. Cut rectangles and squares from cotton fabrics, ⅜" larger all around than area the piece will be sewn to. Use four different yellow prints for spaces #1, #7, and #8. Use cream patterned in spaces #2, #3, #4, #5, #6, #7a, and #8a. Use light green variegated in spaces #9, and #10. Use yellow/orange patterned fabric in space #11.

3. Foundation-piece four Unit As. Sew four Unit As together. Press seam allowances open. (See Illus. A)

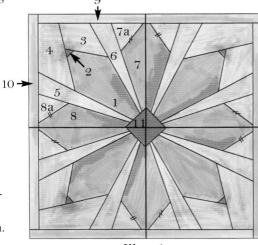

Illus. A

Continued on page 116.

Continued from page 114.

cutting bag fabrics

1. Cut one piece C 23¼" x 14" from cotton batting.

2. Cut one pocket D piece 6½" square from fusible interfacing.

3. Cut two handle pieces E 41" x 3" from yellow/gray/white plaid. Cut four pieces 20" x 2" from fusible interfacing

4. Cut two handle wrap pieces F 3" square from yellow/gray/white plaid.

5. Cut one tab piece G 2" x 4" from yellow/gray/white plaid.

quilting towels

1. Sandwich batting between towels, wrong sides facing, aligning towel outer edges. *Note: The batting is smaller in size than the towels.*

2. Using a free-motion machine-quilting technique in a grid pattern, machine-quilt the layers together, having grids approximately 2¼" apart. Do not sew towels together at outer edges.

making pocket and handles

1. Fuse the interfacing to the wrong side of the pocket lining fabric piece D.

2. Sew the pocket lining to the quilt block, right sides facing, along the top and bottom edges, using a ¼" seam allowance.

3. Turn right side out. Press.

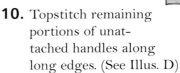

Illus. A

4. Position pocket 4½" down from one 20" towel edge and centered between the towel side edges. *Note: There will be about 6½" on either side of the pocket. (See Illus. A)*

5. Sew pocket in place along sides and bottom edges. *Note: The side edges are not finished at this point.*

6. Fuse interfacing centered to wrong side of each handle. *Note: The interfacing is pieced when fused in place.*

7. Press long handle edges under ½" to wrong side. Press handle in half, aligning pressed-under edges.

8. Using water-soluble fabric-marking pen, mark towel for handle placement by extending pocket placement onto towel. Mark 2¼" from front and back upper towel edges along handle placement line. (See Illus. B)

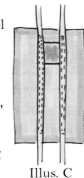

9. Sew handles to towel layers along side edges, enclosing pocket side edges in he process. Sew across handles at 2½" marks. (See Illus. C)

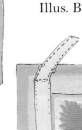

Illus. B

10. Topstitch remaining portions of unattached handles along long edges. (See Illus. D)

Illus. C

Illus. D

applying zipper

1. Pin finished bag front upper edge of towel to left edge of zipper tape, aligning fabric edge to edge of zipper coil, extending zipper across entire upper edge of bag front. Using a zipper foot, machine-sew upper edge to zipper tape. Sew again ⅛" from first row of stitching. Do not catch towel lining in when sewing zipper to bag front upper edge.

2. Align and sew upper edge of bag back to opposite side of zipper tape in the same manner as with Step 1. *Note: It may be helpful to turn the bag inside out when sewing the zipper in place for this step.*

finishing bag

1. With bag inside out, fold bag in half, aligning zipper edges. Mark fold line. Move towel lining away from side edges.

2. Measure and mark 2½" upward from fold line along both side edges of bag. Measure and mark 2½" upward from this set of marks. (See Illus. E)

Illus. E

3. Fold bag on first 2½" mark, bringing bottom folded edge inward and upward to second mark.

4. Pin and stitch sides close to finished towel edges through all layers. (See Illus. F)

Illus. F

5. Measure and mark lining in the same manner as with Step 2 on page 116. With wrong sides facing, fold, pin, and stitch as with Steps 3–4 on page 116.

6. From outside, push side seams out to form soft triangle shape at base of seam line.

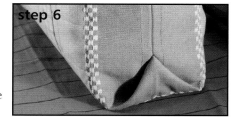

step 6

7. Hand-stitch upper edges of lining to zipper tape.

8. Stitch opening ends closed to hide zipper tape ends.

9. Working with tab piece G, press 4" edges under ½" to wrong side. Press ends under ½" to wrong side. Press piece in half, aligning ends. Machine-sew sides edges together, forming tab.

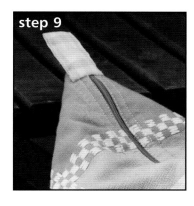

step 9

10. Hand-stitch ends of tab to right end of bag top edges over end of zipper.

11. Working with handles that are on one side of bag, place handle ends with right sides facing. Machine-sew ends together, using a ¼" seam allowance. Press seam allowance open. Repeat for remaining handle ends.

12. Working with handle wrap piece F, press the two parallel edges under ½" to wrong side.

13. Wrap piece around handle seam line. Pin in place.

14. Mark 1¼" on either side of the handle from wrap piece. Fold handle in half between marks. Pin together.

15. Sew handle together between marks through all layers. (See Illus. I)

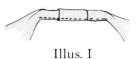

Illus. I

16. Slip ribbon through zipper pull. Tie ribbon ends together. Coat ends with fray preventative. When dry, trim ends at a slant.

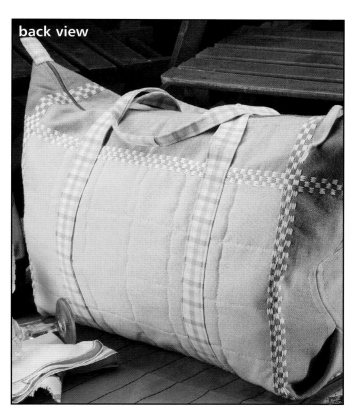

back view

delight pattern

Pattern on this page is actual size.

Unit A

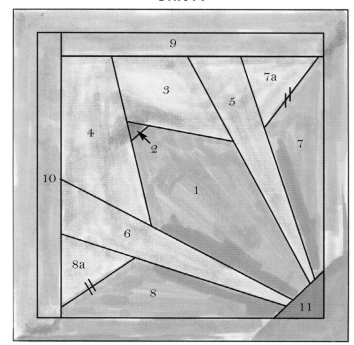

calm & balance

Free from agitation, excitement, or disturbance.

finished size
• 18" x 13½", side 3½"

fabrics
• 44"-wide fusible fleece (⅝ yd) for body front; back A; side B

Blue/green quilting (2 variations)
• 44"-wide blue/green large floral (1 yd) for body front/back lining A; side lining B; squares within squares quilt block
• 44"-wide blue/green striped (⅔ yd) for body front, back A; side B; inside base C; pocket sashings E1, E2; handle wrap H

Green quilting (3 variations)
• 44"-wide dark green wavy striped (⅛ yd) for evening star quilt block
• 44"-wide green polka-dot (⅜ yd) for pocket lining F; quilt blocks
• 44"-wide green mottled print (⅛ yd) for both quilt blocks

Turquoise cottons (2 variations)
• 44"-wide turquoise heavy-weight solid (⅜ yd) for outer base D; handle G
• 44"-wide turquoise small floral quilting cotton (¼ yd) for quilt blocks

notions
• 22"-wide fusible woven interfacing (1½ yds) for body front; back lining A; side lining B; inside base C; handle wrap H
• 22"-wide medium-weight nonwoven interfacing (½ yd) for quilt blocks
• Matching threads

tools
• General Tools on page 5
• Fine-tipped brown permanent ink fabric-marking pen
• Needles: hand-sewing; jeans
• Needle-nosed pliers

cutting fabrics

Note: Seam allowances are ½" unless otherwise noted.

1. Cut two pieces 19" x 14½" for body front and back A from blue/green striped fabric, with stripes running parallel to 14½" edges. Cut two each for body front and back lining A from large floral and fusible interfacing. Cut two from fusible fleece that does not have ½" seam allowance added. *Note: This is done to help eliminate bulk.*

2. Cut two pieces 4½" x 14½" for side B from the blue/green striped fabric, with the stripes running parallel to the 4½" edges. Cut two each for side B lining from the large floral and fusible interfacing. Cut two from the fusible fleece that do not have the ½" seam allowance added.

3. Cut one piece each 19" x 4½" for inside base C from blue/green striped fabric and large floral. Cut two from fusible interfacing.

4. Cut one piece each 21½" x 7½" for outer base D from turquoise heavy-weight cotton and fusible interfacing.

5. Cut four pieces 7" x 3" for pocket sashing E1 from blue/green striped fabric, with stripes running parallel to 3" edges. Cut four pieces 7" x 2" for pocket sashing E2 from blue/green striped fabric, with stripes running parallel to 2" edges.

6. Cut two pieces 25" x 7" for pocket lining F from green polka-dot fabric.

7. Cut two pieces 2½" x 39" for handle G from the turquoise heavy-weight cotton.

8. Cut four pieces 3" x 4½" for handle wrap H from blue/green striped fabric, with stripes running parallel to 3" edges. Cut two pieces from fusible interfacing.

preparing bag pieces

1. Fuse fleece to wrong sides of body front and back A pieces A. Fuse interfacing to body front and back lining A pieces.

2. Fuse fleece to side B pieces B. Fuse interfacing to side lining B pieces.

Continued on page 120.

Continued from page 118.

3. Fuse interfacing to inside base C pieces.

4. Fuse interfacing to outer base D piece.

5. Fuse interfacing to two handle wrap H pieces.

making evening star foundation-pieced quilt block

Refer to Foundation Piecing on pages 7–8 before beginning.

1. Using Unit A for Evening Star Pattern on page 122 for foundation-pieced quilt block, trace 12 onto nonwoven interfacing, using a permanent ink fabric-marking pen and grid-lined ruler.

2. Cut rectangles or squares from quilting cottons ⅜" larger all around than area piece will be sewn to, including excessive seam allowance included on pattern. Use darker green wavy striped for space #1. Use turquoise small floral for spaces #2, and #3. Use green mottled print for space #4. Use green polka-dot for spaces #5 and #6.

3. Foundation-piece 12 Unit As.

4. Trim Unit As along diagonal edges, using a ¼" seam allowance.

5. Sew four Unit As together along diagonal edges, matching at intersections. (See Illus. A) Press seam allowances open.

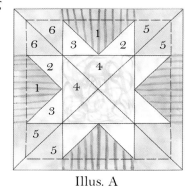

Illus. A

6. Trim assembled blocks along outer edges, using a ½" seam allowance.

7. Repeat Steps 4–6 for remaining eight Unit As.

making squares within squares foundation-pieced quilt blocks

1. Using Unit A for Squares Within Squares Pattern on page 122 for foundation-pieced quilt block, trace three onto nonwoven interfacing, using a permanent ink fabric-marking pen and grid-lined ruler.

2. Cut rectangles or squares from quilting cottons ⅜" larger all around than area piece will be sewn to, including excessive seam allowance included on

the pattern. Use green mottled print for space #1. Use turquoise small floral for spaces #2, #3, #4, and #5. Use green polka-dot for spaces #6, #7, #8, and #9. Use large floral for spaces #10, #11, #12, and #13.

3. Foundation-piece three Unit As.

4. Trim Unit As along outer edges, using a ¼" seam allowance.

sashing blocks together

1. Sew two groups of three blocks together, with sashing along the side edges. Work with two of same block at ends and one contrasting block at the center.

2. Sew 3"-wide pocket sashing pieces E1 to both sides of center block. Press seam allowances open.

3. Sew side blocks to opposite edges of center block sashing pieces. Press seam allowances open.

4. Sew 2"-wide pocket sashing pieces E2 to the ends of outer blocks. Press seam allowances open. (See Illus. B)

Illus. B

5. Repeat Steps 2–4 for other group of three blocks.

making handles

1. Press long edges of handle G pieces under ½" to wrong side. Press in half, aligning pressed-under edges. Pin pressed-under edges together.

2. Measure 11" from either end. Topstitch along both edges in between the 11" measurements.

3. Place an interfaced handle wrap and handle wrap H piece together, with right sides facing.

4. Sew across short ends, using a ¼" seam allowance. Press seam allowances open. Turn right side out. Press flat.

5. Sew longer edges together with right sides facing, using a ¼" seam allowance and forming a tube. Press seam allowance open. Turn tube right side out.

6. Repeat Steps 3–5 for other handle wrap pieces.

7. Slip handle wrap tubes onto each handle, positioning wraps at center of handles.

making outer pockets

1. Sew pocket lining F pieces to sashed quilt block pieces along upper edges, with right sides facing. Press seam allowance toward outer pocket. Fold lining to back side along seam line. Press.

2. Topstitch close to finished edge.

3. Press pockets along sashing seam lines. Topstitch at seam lines through layers to create crisp edges. (See Illus. C)

Illus. C

4. Box-pleat two center sashing spaces by bringing topstitched edges to center of sashing spaces. Press pleats.

5. Form half box pleats at the outer sashing spaces. Press. (See Illus. D)

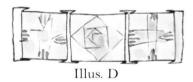

Illus. D

sewing outer pockets and handles to front and back

1. Using water-soluble fabric-marking pen, draw a line on front that is 1" upward from bottom edge. Repeat for back.

2. Position bottom edge of outer pockets on drawn line.

3. Pin pockets to front and back at the side and bottom edges, leaving center pleated spaces unpinned.

4. Working with front, slip end from one handle within space of one center pleat. Slip other end of handle within space of opposite center pleat.

5. Sew handle ends to outer pocket/front up to topstitched portion of handle. Sew across handle and to front at this junction. (See Illus. E)

outer pockets

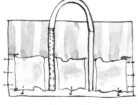

Illus. E

6. Repeat Steps 4–5 for remaining handle and outer pocket/back piece.

7. Pin pleats over handle ends along bottom edge. Machine-baste outer pocket to front and back along sides and bottom edges.

sewing sides to bag body and body lining

1. Sew side B pieces to sides of front and back, aligning the 14½" edges. Press the seam allowances open.

2. Sew side lining B pieces to the sides of the front and back lining A pieces in the same manner as Step 1.

3. Slip assembled lining over assembled bag body with right sides facing, aligning upper edges.

4. Sew around upper edges. Press seam allowance toward lining.

5. Slip lining within bag body. Press top edge flat, allowing a scant edge of lining to show at upper edge.

6. Topstitch around upper edge ¼" from seam line.

7. Fold bag on one side edge seam line. Topstitch close to seam line. Repeat for each side edge seam line. *Note: This will create crisp side edges for the bag.*

sewing inside base pieces to bag bottom

1. Pin together two inside base C pieces, with wrong sides facing.

2. With lining sides facing, sew layered inside bases to bottom edge of bag/lining, working with front and back edges to begin. Sew side edges together.

3. Press seam allowance upward as much as possible. *Note: The seam allowance is on the outside of the bag.*

sewing outer base piece to bag bottom

1. Press long edges of the outer base D piece under ½" to wrong side. Pin one long edge to bag front along bottom edge of outer pocket, using a ½" seam allowance. Continue by pinning excess onto bag sides.

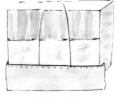

Illus. F

2. Topstitch long edge to front and sides close to pressed-under edge. (See Illus. F)

3. Wrap outer base piece underneath and around to back.

4. Pin other long edge to bag back along bottom edge of outer pocket, continuing excess onto sides. *Note: This step is a bit awkward.* Topstitch as with Step 3.

5. At sides, fold outer edges of outer base upward, folding edges diagonally. Fold upper edge under. Hand-stitch upper edge in place. Repeat for the opposite side.

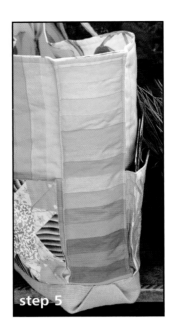

step 5

calm & balance patterns

Enlarge patterns on this page 200%.

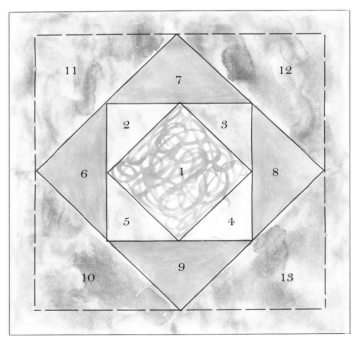

Unit A for Squares Within Squares

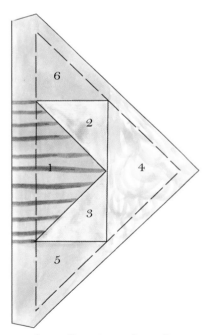

Unit A for Evening Star

familiarity

To have a close acquaintance with something. Frequently seen or experienced. A vigorous exertion of power.

Familiarity photo shown on page 126

finished size
• 19" x 13", side gusset 5"

embellishments
• 8" x 5" bamboo handle with hardware (2)

fabrics
• 44"-wide fusible fleece (1⅛ yds) for Pattern A; Pattern B; side gusset C; zipper strips D

Blue (4 variations)
• 44"-wide blue plaid cotton (1 yd) for Pattern A lining; Pattern B lining; side gusset C lining
• 54"–60"-wide blue/cream floral home dec (⅞ yd) for side gusset C; zipper strips D, Pattern E; zipper pull

Cream (2 variations)
• 54"–60"-wide cream/yellow/blue striped home dec (½ yd) for Pattern A; Pattern B for back pocket

Solids (3 variations)
•55"–60"-wide pale yellow, cream, chambray cotton solids with texture (¼ yd) for quilt blocks

notions
• 22"-wide fusible woven interfacing (½ yd) for side gusset C; zipper strips D
• 22"-wide medium-weight nonwoven inter-facing (⅛ yd) for quilt block
• 24" cream heavy-weight nylon zipper
• Matching threads

tools
• General Tools on page 5
• Needle-nosed pliers
• Needles: hand-sewing; jeans

cutting fabrics
Note: Enlarge Familiarity Patterns on page 127 200% unless otherwise indicated.

1. Using Pattern A, cut two each for front and back from cream/yellow/blue striped and blue plaid fabrics, having stripes vertically aligned. Cut two from fusible fleece that does not have ½" seam allowance added. *Note: This is done to help eliminate bulk.*

2. Using Pattern B, cut one from cream/yellow/blue striped fabric, having stripes horizontally aligned. Cut two from blue plaid fabric. Cut two from fusible fleece that does not have ½" seam allowance added.

3. Cut one side gusset C each from blue/cream floral, blue plaid, and fusible interfacing (piece as necessary). Cut one piece 27¼" x 5" from fusible fleece.

4. Cut two zipper strips D from blue/cream floral. Cut two pieces 24¼" x 2¾" from the fusible interfacing (piece as necessary). Cut two pieces 23¼" x 2¼" from fusible fleece.

5. Using Pattern E, cut two tabs from the blue/cream floral fabric.

6. Cut four 3"-square handle loops F from blue/cream floral fabric.

7. Cut one zipper pull G 1" x 10" from the blue/cream floral fabric.

8. Using water-soluble fabric-marking pen, mark all fabric pieces as indicated with the pattern assembly markings. Refer to pattern pieces when assembling each bag.

making foundation-pieced quilt block
Refer to Foundation Piecing on pages 7–8 before beginning. Do not trim the excess away from the outer edges of the blocks until indicated in the directions.

1. Using Unit A pattern for foundation-pieced quilt block, trace eight Unit As onto nonwoven interfacing, using water-soluble fabric-marking pen and grid-lined ruler.

2. Using Unit B Pattern, trace eight Unit Bs onto nonwoven interfacing in the same manner. Be certain to add seam allowance to each traced piece.

3. For Unit A, cut rectangles or squares from textured cotton fabrics ⅜" larger all around than the area piece will be sewn to, including excessive seam allowance included on pattern. Use cream for space #1. Use yellow for space #2. Use chambray for space #3.

4. For Unit B, cut rectangles in the same manner as in Step 3. Use chambray for space #1. Use yellow for space #2. Use cream for space #3.

5. Foundation-piece eight Unit As and eight Unit Bs. Sew Unit As to Unit Bs. (See Illus. A) Press seam allowances open.

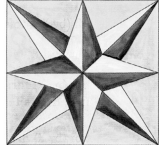
Illus. A

6. Sew four assembled units together to make one quilt block. Repeat for remaining four assembled units.

7. Place two assembled quilt blocks side by side. Trim right edge of block that is on left side, using a ¼" seam allowance. Trim left edge of block that is on right side, using a ¼" seam allowance. Sew trimmed edges together, using a ¼" seam allowance. Press seam allowance open.

8. Using pattern B, cut sewn-together quilt blocks into the outer pocket shape. *Note: This piece is quite bulky.*

making outer pockets

1. Fuse fleece centered to wrong sides of B outer pocket pieces. *Note: One is foundation-pieced and the other is the striped fabric piece.*

outer pocket

2. Pin the outer pockets to pocket lining pieces, right sides facing. Sew the upper edges together, using a ¼" seam allowance. Press seam allowance toward outer pocket. Fold the lining to the back side along the seam line and press.

3. Topstitch ¼" from finished edge.

4. Machine-baste sides and bottom edges of the outer pockets to pocket lining, using a ⅜" seam allowance.

5. Fuse fusible fleece centered to wrong sides of front and back pieces.

6. Place front and back lining pieces against fleece side of front and back. Pin together at edges. Machine-baste around edges of layered front and layered back pieces, using a ⅜" seam allowance.

7. Layer outer pockets onto front and back pieces. Machine-baste layers together along side and bottom edges. Topstitch top edge of pockets to front and back pieces 1½" inward from side edges.

8. Working with handle loop F pieces, press parallel edges under ½" to the wrong side. Press in half, aligning pressed-under edges. Sew along both the edges.

9. Fold two handle loop pieces in half, matching short ends. Pin ends to top edge of front where handle loop placement is indicated on pattern. Repeat for remaining two handle loop pieces and top edge of back.

making side gusset

1. Fuse fusible fleece to wrong side of side gusset C blue/cream floral piece. Fuse fusible interfacing to wrong side of blue plaid piece.

2. Place two side gussets together, with wrong sides facing. Pin along the outer edges. Machine-baste outer edges together, using a ⅜" seam allowance.

3. Fold side gusset in half, matching the short ends. Mark center top and bottom edges at fold.

4. Press one zipper strip D in half, wrong sides facing, aligning long edges. Fuse interfacing to one half of zipper strip, beginning at inner fold. Fuse fusible fleece to other half of zipper strip, beginning at inner fold. Repeat for other zipper strip D.

5. Press strips in half, wrong sides facing, aligning long edges.

6. Fold strips in half, matching short ends. Mark center top and bottom raw edges at fold.

7. Pin folded edge of one zipper strip to left edge of the zipper tape, aligning fabric edge to edge of zipper coil. Using a zipper foot, sew upper edge to zipper tape. Sew again ⅜" from first row of stitching.

8. Align and sew edge of remaining zipper strip to opposite side of the zipper tape in the same manner as with Step 7.

9. Place two tab E pieces, with right sides facing. Sew side and curved edges, using a ¼" seam allowance. Clip seam allowance at curve to seam line. Edge-press seam allowance open. Turn right side out. Press.

10. With zipper closed, pin tab onto right end of zipper strips, with right sides facing.

11. Sew side gusset to zipper strips at short ends. Press seam allowances toward side gusset. Do not stitch through zipper teeth.

12. Topstitch seam allowance ¼" from seam line onto side gusset.

back view

sewing gusset to front and back

1. Pin and sew side gusset/zipper strips to front, with right sides facing, matching center front along top and bottom edges, using a ½" seam allowance. Work from side gusset/zipper strips side when sewing. Clip side gusset/zipper strips to seam line along curved edges of bag front. Press seam allowance toward side gusset/zipper strips.

side view

2. Sew again ⅛" from first row of stitching. Trim seam allowance just past the second row of stitching. Overcast seam allowance with a tight zigzag stitch.

3. Repeat Steps 1–2 for bag back, making certain to open zipper a bit in order to turn bag right side out.

finishing

1. Using handle hardware, attach the bamboo handles to back through loops at front and back top edges.

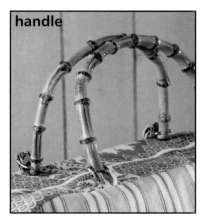

handle

2. Working with zipper pull G piece, press long edges under ¼" to wrong side. Press in half, aligning pressed-under edges. Sew layers together along pressed-under edges.

3. Slip zipper pull fabric piece through the zipper pull. Sew layers together. Coat ends with fray preventative. When dry, cut ends at a slant.

familiarity patterns

Enlarge patterns on this page as indicated.

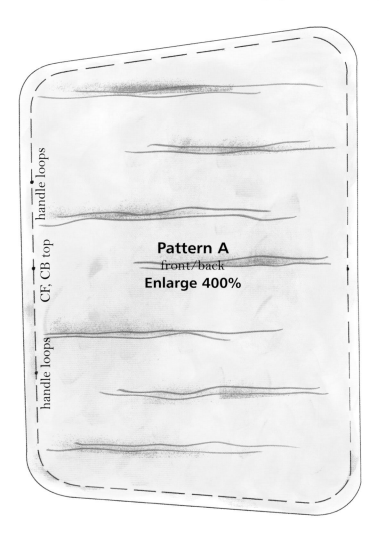

Pattern A
front/back
Enlarge 400%

handle loops

CF, CB top

handle loops

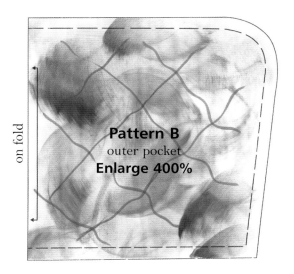

on fold

Pattern B
outer pocket
Enlarge 400%

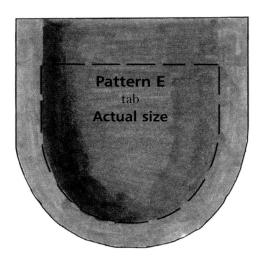

Pattern E
tab
Actual size

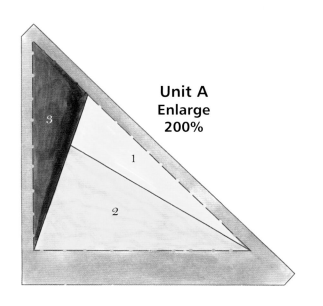

Unit A
Enlarge
200%

3

1

2

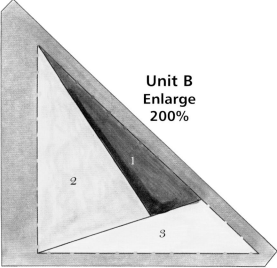

Unit B
Enlarge
200%

1

2

3

warmth & beauty

A glowing effect that is produced by the use of warm colors.

finished size
- 20" x 15"

embellishments
- 1⅜"-wide brass button with jeweled center
- 1½"-wide jacquard trim (⅜ yd)
- 12" x 4" wooden handles with slat along straight edge (2)

fabrics
- 44"-wide fusible fleece (⅝ yd) for Pattern A; Pattern D; Pattern G
- 54"-wide black/brown striped silk brocade (⅜ yd) for Pattern B; E inner pockets
- 54"-wide black/brown/taupe cotton chenille (½ yd) for lining A
- 54"-wide brown/taupe cotton chenille (¼ yd) for Pattern C
- 54"-wide cream/black satin matelassé (⅞ yd) for Pattern A lining, Pattern D lining; handle strips F, Pattern G

notions
- 22"-wide woven fusible interfacing (⅞ yd) for Pattern D; inner pocket E; handle strip F
- Matching threads

tools
- General Tools on page 5
- Needles: hand-sewing; jeans

cutting fabrics

Note: Enlarge Warmth & Beauty Patterns on pages 132–133 200% unless otherwise indicated.

1. Using Pattern A, cut two each for front and back from black/brown/taupe chenille and cream with black satin matelassé (for lining). Cut two from fusible fleece that does not have the ½" seam allowance added. *Note: This is done to help eliminate bulk.*

2. Using Pattern B, cut one outer pocket top strip from black/brown striped brocade.

3. Using Pattern C, cut one outer pocket bottom strip from brown/taupe chenille.

4. Using Pattern D, cut two from the cream with black satin matelassé. Cut one from the fusible interfacing. Cut one from the fusible fleece that does not have the ½" seam allowance added.

5. Cut two inner pockets E 15" x 16" from black/brown brocade striped and fusible interfacing.

6. Cut two handle strips F each 11" x 3" from cream/black satin matelassé (outer pieces), black/brown striped brocade (lining pieces) and fusible interfacing.

7. Using pattern G, cut one outer pocket lining each from cream with black satin matelassé and fusible interfacing. Cut one from fusible fleece that does not have the ½" seam allowance added.

8. Using water-soluble marking-pen, mark all fabric pieces as indicated with the pattern assembly markings. Refer to pattern pieces when assembling each bag. *Note: All seam allowances are ½".*

Continued on page 130.

Continued from page 128.

making outer pocket

1. Sew outer pocket top and bottom strips together where indicated on the pattern, right sides facing. Press seam allowance open.

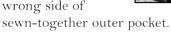
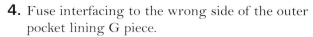

2. Sew jacquard trim to seam line between top and bottom strips.

3. Fuse fusible fleece centered to the wrong side of sewn-together outer pocket.

4. Fuse interfacing to the wrong side of the outer pocket lining G piece.

5. Pin outer pocket to outer pocket lining piece, right sides facing. Sew the upper edges together. Press seam allowance toward outer pocket. Fold lining to back side along seam line. Press.

6. Topstitch close to seam line along outer pocket upper edge.

7. Using a free-motion machine-quilt along the brocade stripes and jacquard trim.

8. Layer outer pocket onto front piece. Machine-baste layers together along the sides and the bottom edges.

sewing front to back

1. Place front and back together, right sides facing, aligning side and bottom edges.

2. Sew sides together. Press seam allowances open.

3. Sew bottom edges together. Press seam allowance open.

4. To make corners, fold one end from bottom seam line so that it meets end of adjacent side seam, with right sides facing. Pin in place. Repeat for remaining ends.

5. Sew across the corners. Press seam allowances.

making flap

1. Fuse interfacing to wrong side of one flap D piece. Fuse fleece centered to wrong side of other flap D piece.

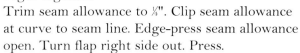

2. Place the flaps with right sides facing.

3. Sew side and bottom curved edges together. Trim seam allowance to ¼". Clip seam allowance at curve to seam line. Edge-press seam allowance open. Turn flap right side out. Press.

4. Make a buttonhole on the flap where indicated on the pattern.

5. Pin upper edge of flap centered to center-top edge of back, right sides facing.

sewing handle strips to front and back

1. Fuse interfacing to wrong side of handle strips F outer fabric pieces.

2. Sew outer handle strip pieces to lining handle strip pieces, right sides facing, along short ends. Press seam allowances toward outer fabric pieces. Turn right side out. Press.

3. Pin one long edge of handle strip piece centered to center-top edge of back, right sides facing.

4. Slip other long edge of handle strip piece through wooden handle slat, then pin this edge to center top edge of back on top of edge from Step 3. (See Illus. A)

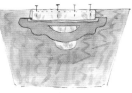

Illus. A

5. Machine-baste handle strip to back, using a ⅜" seam allowance.

making inner pockets

1. Fuse interfacing to wrong sides of inner pocket E fabric pieces.

2. Fold one pocket in half, aligning the 15" edges, with right sides facing.

3. Sew side edges together. Clip bulk from corner. Edge-press seam allowances open. Turn right side out. Press.

4. Repeat Steps 2–3 for second pocket.

5. Press remaining raw edge of pockets under ½".

making lining

1. Fuse fusible fleece centered to wrong side of lining front and back pieces.

2. Pin pockets to lining front and back pieces where indicated on Pattern A. *Note: The folded edge is the top edge of the pocket. The pressed-under edge is the bottom pocket edge.*

3. Sew pockets to lining front and back along sides and bottom edges, as well as diagonally as indicated on Pattern A.

4. Sew lining front and back together. Follow **sewing front to back**, Steps 1–5 on page 130. At Step 3, leave a 12" opening along bottom-edge seam line in order to turn bag right side out.

finishing

1. Slip lining over bag, with right sides facing. Align top edges.

2. Sew lining to bag around top edges. *Note: The wooden handle is rigid to work with, but manageable.*

3. Press seam allowance toward outer bag fabric.

4. Turn bag right side out through lining seam opening.

5. Topstitch top edge of bag ¼" from finished edge.

6. Hand-stitch lining opening closed.

7. Stitch button to outer pocket where indicated on Pattern B.

warmth & beauty patterns

Enlarge patterns on this page 400%.

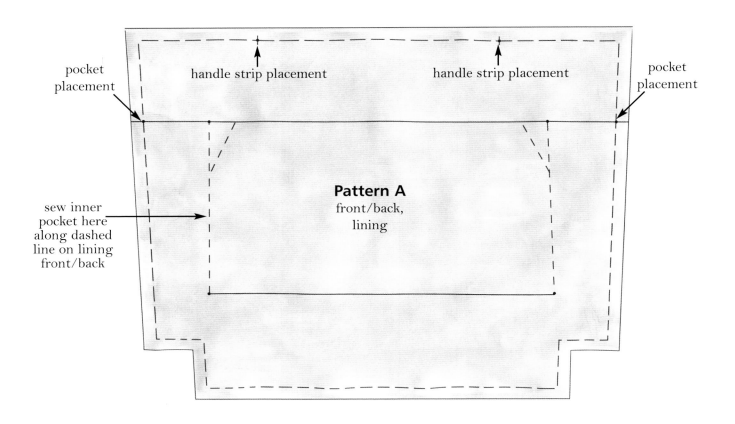

pocket
placement

handle strip placement

handle strip placement

pocket
placement

sew inner
pocket here
along dashed
line on lining
front/back

Pattern A
front/back,
lining

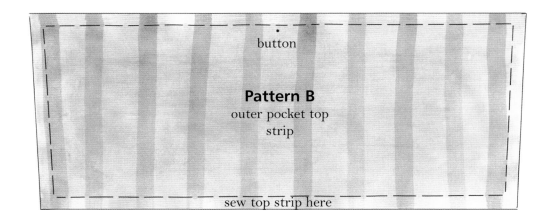

button

Pattern B
outer pocket top
strip

sew top strip here

warmth & beauty patterns

Enlarge patterns on this page as indicated.

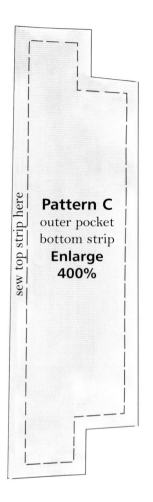

Pattern C
outer pocket
bottom strip
**Enlarge
400%**

sew top strip here

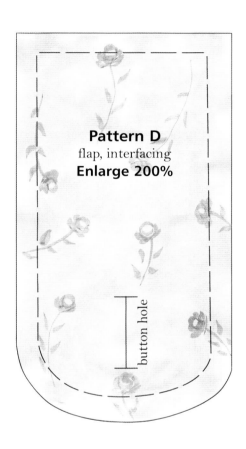

Pattern D
flap, interfacing
Enlarge 200%

button hole

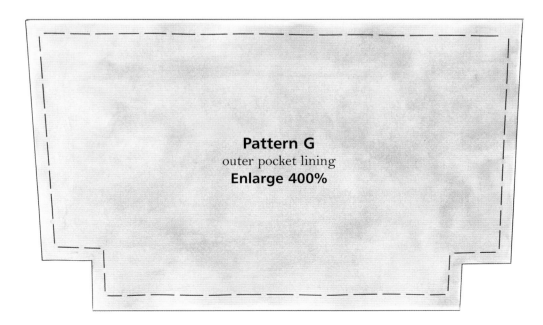

Pattern G
outer pocket lining
Enlarge 400%

joy

An emotion evoked by well-being, success, or good fortune.

finished size
- 18" x 14", side gusset 4"

embellishments
- 1" red button
- ⅜"-wide ivory ribbon (6")
- Embroidery flosses: dark gold; red

fabrics
- 44"-wide fusible fleece (⅝ yd)

Ecru (1 variation)
- Ecru textured cotton flannel (3" x 4") for Chef Appliqués #1, #5, #6

Gold (2 variations)
- 54"-wide gold/cream striped home deco (½ yd) for Pattern A; Pattern D
- Gold textured wool felt (3" x 1") for Chef Appliqué #10

Ivory (3 variations)
- 44"–54"-wide ivory textured cotton (¼ yd) for pieced side gusset E; Basket appliqué #1; chef appliqué #8
- Ivory textured cotton (5" x 4") for chef appliqués #2, #7
- Ivory tulle (20" x 16") for Pattern A appliqué overlay

Red (4 variations)
- 44"-wide red cotton broadcloth (¼ yd) for pieced side gusset E; Basket Appliqués #2, #3, #4; Chef Appliqués #4, #9; shirt trim
- 44"-wide red striped cotton (⅜ yd) for Pattern B; side binding G; top binding H; flap binding I; Basket Appliqués #5, #6, #7; Chef Appliqué #3
- 54"-wide red/gold checkered home deco (1 yd) for Pattern A lining; Pattern C; side gusset lining F
- Red wool felt (3" x 1") for Chef Appliqué #11

notions
- ⅜" snap
- Threads: dark brown; matching

tools
- General Tools on page 5
- Embroidery needles: sizes 3, 5
- Tacky glue

cutting fabrics

Note: Enlarge Joy Patterns on pages 138–141 200% unless otherwise indicated.

1. Using Pattern A for front and back, cut two from cream/gold striped fabric. Cut two for front and back lining from red/gold checkered fabric. Cut two from fusible fleece that does not have the ½" seam allowance added. *Note: This is done to help eliminate bulk.*

2. Using Pattern B for handle, cut four from red striped fabric. Cut two from fusible interfacing.

3. Using Pattern C for inner pleated pocket, cut two from red/gold checkered fabric.

4. Using Pattern D for flap, cut two from cream/gold striped fabric. Cut one from fleece that does not have ½" seam allowance added.

5. Cut twenty-two 3" squares each for the pieced side gusset E from the red broadcloth and 44"–54"-wide ivory textured fabric.

6. Cut one 45" x 5" for side gusset lining F from red/gold checkered fabric and one from fleece. Do not add ½" seam allowance on fleece piece.

7. Cut two 45" x 2" pieces for side binding G from red striped fabric.

8. Cut one 45" x 2" piece for top binding H from red striped fabric.

Continued on page 136.

9. Cut one 22" x 2" for flap binding I from red striped fabric.

10. Using water-soluble fabric-marking pen, mark all fabric pieces as indicated with the pattern assembly markings. Refer to pattern pieces when assembling each bag. *Note: Seam allowances are ½" unless otherwise noted.*

Appliquéd front cutting technique:

11. Cut out each shape along outlines.

12. Place appliqué pattern pieces with their corresponding fabrics. Spray starch each piece of fabric for amount needed to cut out appliqué pieces.

13. Using water-soluble fabric-marking pen, trace the appliqué pieces face down onto each piece of fabric.

14. Cut out appliqué pieces from fabrics as indicated below:

a. Using Basket Appliqué Pattern #1, cut one from 44"–54"-wide ivory textured fabric.

b. Using Basket Appliqué Pattern #2, cut eight from red broadcloth.

c. Using Basket Appliqué Pattern #3, cut six from red broadcloth.

d. Cut one strip ⅛" x 7¼" along bias for Basket Appliqué #4 from red broadcloth.

e. Using Basket Appliqué Patterns #5, #6, and #7, cut one of each from the red striped fabric.

f. Using Chef Appliqué Patterns #1, #5, and #6, cut one of each from ecru flannel.

g. Using Chef Appliqué Patterns #2 and #7, cut one of each from ivory textured fabric.

h. Using Chef Appliqué Pattern #3, cut one from red striped fabric.

i. Cut three ¼" squares from red broadcloth for Chef Appliqué Pattern #4.

j. Using Chef Appliqué Pattern #9, cut one from red broadcloth.

k. Cut two strips ⅛" x 4" along bias for chef's shirt trim from red broadcloth.

l. Using Chef Appliqué Pattern #8, cut one from 44"–54"-wide ivory textured fabric.

m. Using Chef Appliqué Pattern #10, cut one from gold wool felt.

n. Using Chef Appliqué Pattern #11, cut one from red wool felt.

appliquéing and quilting front

1. Using water-soluble fabric-marking pen, transfer some of the design placement lines onto cream/gold striped front piece. Using very small finger-dabs of glue, adhere basket appliqué pieces to front in numerical order. (See Illus. A & B)

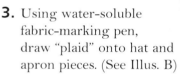

Illus. A

2. Adhere chef appliqué pieces to front in numerical order except for pie-filling piece #11. (See Illus. B) *Note: This piece is hand-stitched in place later.*

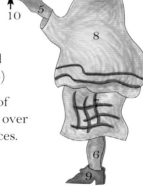
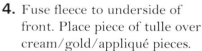

3. Using water-soluble fabric-marking pen, draw "plaid" onto hat and apron pieces. (See Illus. B)

4. Fuse fleece to underside of front. Place piece of tulle over cream/gold/appliqué pieces.

5. Using a free-motion machine-quilting technique, machine-quilt around appliqué pieces.

Illus. B

6. Machine-quilt around outer edges of appliqué pieces with dark brown thread, creating a thin "drawn" outline effect. Machine-quilt "plaid" on hat and apron piece.

7. Trim away excess tulle from front edges.

embroidering details onto appliquéd front

1. Using Backstitch on page 9, embroider flower stems for basket with six strands of red floss. Embroider eyebrow, lips, and pie steam for chef with three strands of red floss.

2. Stitch pie-filling appliqué piece #11 in place.

3. Using French Knot on page 9, embroider eye for chef with three strands of red floss.

4. Using Backstitch, embroider teeth for chef appliqué with three strands of gold floss.

5. Using Couching Stitch on page 9, embroider "plaid" for chef's hat and apron with three stands of gold floss.

making pieced side gusset

1. Sew one of red broadcloth pieced side gusset E pieces to one ivory textured pieced side gusset E piece, right sides facing, using a ½" seam allowance. Press seam allowance toward red broadcloth.

2. Repeat Step 1 twenty-one times for remaining pieced side gusset E pieces.

3. Sew sets together to create checkerboard. Press seam allowances open.

4. Fuse fleece to wrong side of pieced side gusset.

5. Layer side gusset lining F piece to pieced side gusset, with wrong sides facing. Pin together along edges and machine-baste, using a ⅜" seam allowance.

making inner pleated pockets

1. Machine-overcast side and bottom edges of inner pleated pocket pieces.

2. Working with one pocket piece, press side and bottom edges under ½" to wrong side.

3. Press top edge under 1" to wrong side. Machine-hem top edge, turning raw edge under ¼" while hemming.

4. Using water-soluble fabric-marking pen, mark the sides and bottom edges 1¼" from pressed-under edges. Press side and bottom edges along marked line, with wrong sides facing.

side view

inner pleated pocket

5. Pleat bottom edge up to marked and pressed line along bottom of pocket.

6. Pleat side edges up to marked and pressed lines along sides of pocket, keeping pleat along pocket bottom while pleating sides.

7. Repeat Steps 2–6 for remaining pocket piece.

8. Pin one pocket to front lining where indicated on pattern. *Note: The pressed-under edges are the edges to be pinned in place while keeping the pressed pleat folded. The fabric will be very bulky at the bottom corners.*

9. Sew pocket to front lining along sides edges.

10. Sew pocket to front lining along bottom edge.

11. Repeat Steps 9–10 for remaining pleated pocket.

12. Pin one end of piece of ⅜"-wide ribbon to back lining along center of top edge. Machine-baste in place, using a ⅜" seam allowance.

13. Turn other end of ribbon under two times, using a ½" seam allowance. Sew one side of snap to turned-under end of ribbon. Sew the other side of snap to back pocket, centered and 1¼" from hemmed pocket edge.

14. Sew center of front pleated pocket to front lining where indicated on pattern.

sewing side gusset to front and back

1. Fuse the fleece to wrong side of back.

2. Pin and sew side gusset to front, with wrong sides facing, matching center fronts along bottom edge. Work from side-gusset side when pinning and sewing. Clip side gusset to seam line along curved edges of front.

3. Press one side binding G strip in half, aligning long edges.

4. Sew binding strip to front/side gusset along seam line, clipping binding to seam line along curved edges of front.

5. Sew again a scant ⅛" from first row of stitching. Trim seam allowance just past second row of stitching.

6. Fold binding strip over and around seam allowance. Pin in place. Topstitch binding in place to enclose the seam allowance, working from the folded-over side.

7. Repeat Steps 2–6 for back.

making flap

1. Fuse fleece to wrong side of one flap piece.

2. Place two flaps, with wrong sides facing.

3. Bind side and curved edges of flap in the same manner as was done to bind side gusset/front and back seam lines, using flap binding strip I.

4. Make buttonhole on flap where indicated on the pattern.

5. Pin flap to back, centered along top edge, with right sides facing. Machine-baste in place, using a ⅜" seam allowance.

making handles

1. Fuse interfacing to wrong sides of two handle B pieces.

2. Place one interfaced handle and one without interfacing together, with right sides facing.

3. Sew handles together, leaving opening where indicated on pattern.

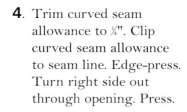
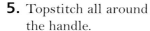

4. Trim curved seam allowance to ¼". Clip curved seam allowance to seam line. Edge-press. Turn right side out through opening. Press.

5. Topstitch all around the handle.

6. Fold handle in half, aligning long edges. Topstitch handle between the dots on pattern along sides and across ends.

7. Sew curved ends of handle to front where indicated on pattern.

8. Repeat Steps 2–7 with remaining handle pieces.

finishing

1. Bind top edge of bag in the same manner as was done to bind side gusset/front and back seam lines, using top binding strip H. Begin and end at center back.

2. Hand-stitch button in place on front.

joy pattern

Enlarge pattern on this page 400%.

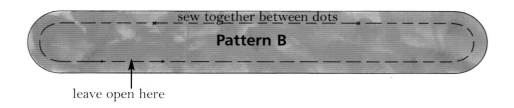

sew together between dots

Pattern B

leave open here

joy patterns

Enlarge patterns on this page 400%.

handle   handle

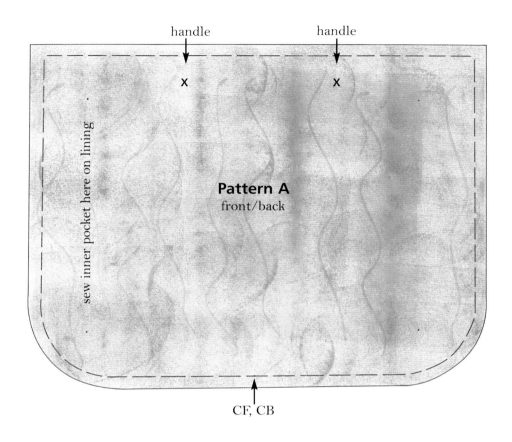

X   X

sew inner pocket here on lining

Pattern A
front/back

CF, CB

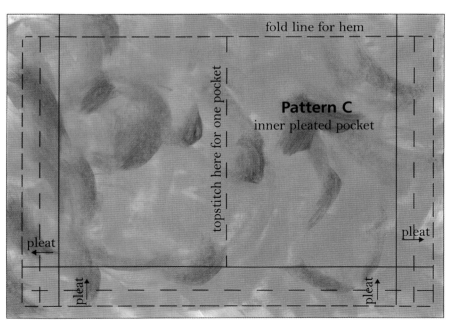

fold line for hem

topstitch here for one pocket

Pattern C
inner pleated pocket

pleat

pleat

pleat

pleat

joy patterns

Enlarge patterns on this page as indicated.

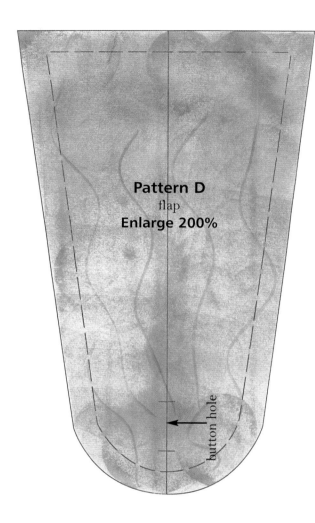

Pattern D
flap
Enlarge 200%

button hole

**Basket Appliqué
Pattern #4**

Enlarge 200%

**Basket Appliqué
Pattern #1
Enlarge 200%**

**Basket
Appliqué
Pattern #2**
Actual size

**Basket
Appliqué
Pattern #3**
Actual size

**Basket Appliqué
Pattern #5**
Actual size

**Basket Appliqué
Pattern #6**
Actual size

**Basket
Appliqué
Pattern #7**
Actual size

joy patterns

Patterns on this page are actual size.

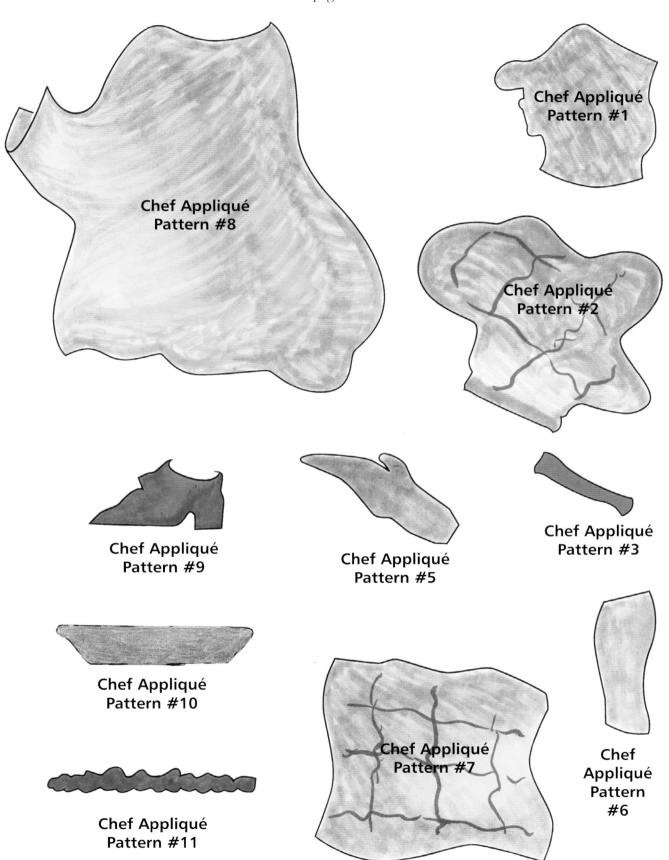

Chef Appliqué Pattern #1

Chef Appliqué Pattern #8

Chef Appliqué Pattern #2

Chef Appliqué Pattern #9

Chef Appliqué Pattern #5

Chef Appliqué Pattern #3

Chef Appliqué Pattern #10

Chef Appliqué Pattern #7

Chef Appliqué Pattern #6

Chef Appliqué Pattern #11

about the author

A short history or biographical information about the writer of this book.

Mary Jo Hiney has been an author with Sterling/Chapelle since 1992 and this book is her 17th offering in collaboration with the teams at Sterling Publishing and Chapelle, Ltd,.—opportunities for which she is filled with gratitude. As a freelance designer, Mary Jo also contributes her design skills to other enterprises in the fabric and craft industry, including her own.

Mary Jo has a love for fabric and sewing that she credits to her mom, when, as a child, together they would visit the local fabric store and savor the loveliness in each bolt of fabric and the excitement for the project in mind. Mary Jo was taught the art of quilting by her sister, Rose, who continues to inspire her and with whom she can discuss ideas and get excellent creative advice. Mary Jo lives with her family on the treasured Central Coast of California.

Dedication:
For my brothers: Ricky and Frankie

Acknowledgement:
I would like to take this opportunity to express my gratitude to my editor, Karmen, for her careful work, for clearly and artfully organizing the information that is poured into this book. I would also like to thank Kim, Areta, and my niece Lauren for their loving contributions. I continue to be grateful to my dear friends at Chapelle for their dedicated work on my behalf. Special thanks to following companies for supplying the products used in this book: The Cotton Ball; Hoffman California Fabrics; Prym/Dritz Corporation; and Quilter's Resource.

metric conversion charts

A tabular sheet showing the change from one type of measurement to another.

mm-millimetres cm-centimetres
inches to millimetres and centimetres

inches	mm	cm	inches	cm	inches	cm
1/8	3	0.3	9	22.9	30	76.2
1/4	6	0.6	10	25.4	31	78.7
3/8	10	1.0	11	27.9	32	81.3
1/2	13	1.3	12	30.5	33	83.8
5/8	16	1.6	13	33.0	34	86.4
3/4	19	1.9	14	35.6	35	88.9
7/8	22	2.2	15	38.1	36	91.4
1	25	2.5	16	40.6	37	94.0
1 1/4	32	3.2	17	43.2	38	96.5
1 1/2	38	3.8	18	45.7	39	99.1
1 3/4	44	4.4	19	48.3	40	101.6
2	51	5.1	20	50.8	41	104.1
2 1/2	64	6.4	21	53.3	42	106.7
3	76	7.6	22	55.9	43	109.2
3 1/2	89	8.9	23	58.4	44	111.8
4	102	10.2	24	61.0	45	114.3
4 1/2	114	11.4	25	63.5	46	116.8
5	127	12.7	26	66.0	47	119.4
6	152	15.2	27	68.6	48	121.9
7	178	17.8	28	71.1	49	124.5
8	203	20.3	29	73.7	50	127.0

yards to metres

yards	metres	yards	metres	yards	metres	yards	metres	yards	metres
1/8	0.11	2 1/8	1.94	4 1/8	3.77	6 1/8	5.60	8 1/8	7.43
1/4	0.23	2 1/4	2.06	4 1/4	3.89	6 1/4	5.72	8 1/4	7.54
3/8	0.34	2 3/8	2.17	4 3/8	4.00	6 3/8	5.83	8 3/8	7.66
1/2	0.46	2 1/2	2.29	4 1/2	4.11	6 1/2	5.94	8 1/2	7.77
5/8	0.57	2 5/8	2.40	4 5/8	4.23	6 5/8	6.06	8 5/8	7.89
3/4	0.69	2 3/4	2.51	4 3/4	4.34	6 3/4	6.17	8 3/4	8.00
7/8	0.80	2 7/8	2.63	4 7/8	4.46	6 7/8	6.29	8 7/8	8.12
1	0.91	3	2.74	5	4.57	7	6.40	9	8.23
1 1/8	1.03	3 1/8	2.86	5 1/8	4.69	7 1/8	6.52	9 1/8	8.34
1 1/4	1.14	3 1/4	2.97	5 1/4	4.80	7 1/4	6.63	9 1/4	8.46
1 3/8	1.26	3 3/8	3.09	5 3/8	4.91	7 3/8	6.74	9 3/8	8.57
1 1/2	1.37	3 1/2	3.20	5 1/2	5.03	7 1/2	6.86	9 1/2	8.69
1 5/8	1.49	3 5/8	3.31	5 5/8	5.14	7 5/8	6.97	9 5/8	8.80
1 3/4	1.60	3 3/4	3.43	5 3/4	5.26	7 3/4	7.09	9 3/4	8.92
1 7/8	1.71	3 7/8	3.54	5 7/8	5.37	7 7/8	7.20	9 7/8	9.03

index

An alphabetical list of items found at the back of a book that states the page number where it can be found.